ENDORSEMENTS

David became a hero when he killed a giant named Goliath with a single stone and presented his head to a king who didn't have the courage to put on his own armor. An act of heroism is when someone reveals through their life what is possible. Through the lens of their life you suddenly see a way that wasn't there before. This book that Jason has written is the language of heroes.

Jason is my friend and he makes me want to be a better dad, husband, friend, and son. When I'm with him and his family, I become better at loving. He is a great storyteller, but more than that, Jason is a good man. He's a personal hero because through his life I see more of what is possible. Real heroes don't make you ache for what you are not. They reveal to you who you are and what you're supposed to be. *Prone to Love* reads as a revelation of who you are becoming. This isn't just Jason's story. It is mine and it is yours. We are all becoming surer of the Father's love.

SCOTT CROWDER
Leader of DreamHouse Church in Newport News, Virginia
www.JesusLoves757.com

I know Jason as a brother, and I love his paradigm of an "always good" God that is captured in this book. He gives us permission to access the Father through his own journey in a lighthearted, easygoing, and conversational manner. Jason writes about the process of his gradual revelation of God's focused affection on us. I am grateful for his ability to express the Father's perfect love toward us as sons and daughters in his book, *Prone to Love*.

ANTHONY SKINNER
Songwriter, Worship Leader, and Author of *WORSHIP SMARTbook*

In *Prone to Love*, Jason does a brilliant job of revealing the truths of Christ's love through Scripture and packaging them in real, humorous, and relatable life stories. As a friend for ten years, I have had the joy of seeing many of these truths played out in his life. While reading this book, I was led to times in my life when God intentionally made His presence known to me, which resulted in strengthening my relationship with Him. The revelations in this book are both timeless and for everyone. You can't read *Prone to Love* and not recall the goodness of God in your own life.

SHAWN RING
Executive Pastor, Spiritual Life Technology, Gateway Church

Most Christian books are instructional. A select few are revelation. And even less are revolutionary. *Prone to Love* is all three and has challenged me to the core. It's brought into question some of the very foundations of what I thought I believed. Jason is living in a love relationship with God that doesn't smell, act, or sound even remotely like religion. There is no works, striving, or pleading—no desperation for God. There is no insecurity in his relationship with God, and that makes me nervous. How can someone be in a relationship with God and not be insecure? Yet when I think about it, what healthy relationship has insecurity at its core? I want what Jason has. I plan to read this book again and again as the revolution grows in my heart.

JOEL N. CLARK
Author of *Awake*

The thing about Jason Clark is that he is dangerous. He is thinking and saying things about God that are turning over the tables of status quo Christianity. And frankly, I like that. In fact, what he is saying in his new book, *Prone to Love*, will probably cause him more trouble than he wants. But Jason is no rabble-rouser. He is a man who has discovered that knowing God is easy and good, and that being loved by God is way simpler than religion has proposed.

Prone to Love dares to suggest that the current relationship status between God and us is way, way better than we could dare to imagine. I believe that Jason's words in this book are groundbreaking and ahead of their time, and yet for many of us, right on time. As you read *Prone to Love*, your theology may be challenged, the way you view God may be shaken, and the way you look at yourself may be changed for the rest of your life. Let it be so!

ANDY SQUYRES
Singer/Songwriter

There are many truths and experiences that will change our lives, but there is no truth or experience that will alter us as deeply as knowing God, the Father. It anchors identity, promises intimacy, and guarantees destiny. Equally relevant are the journeys and stories that bring us face to face with knowing the Father. In *Prone to Love,* Jason Clark does a wonderful job of unmasking the false self while unveiling an extravagant Father. His experiences and ruminations are delightful, stimulating and challenging. I loved the fact that I found myself in many of his stories. This book is a great asset to anyone who is serious about living His Kingdom everywhere.

DR. BILL BENNOT
Pastor of Journey of Grace in Cape Town, South Africa
Author of *Church Planter, Revivalist and Leadership Developer*

Sometimes a story is written that changes everything. This book is an irresistible journey into transforming love. These are new and powerful thoughts from a modern day revivalist. Once they take hold they won't let go.

MARK BATTERSON
Author of *The Circle Maker*

Reading Jason Clark's recent book, *Prone to Love*, will give you a window into the human heart. At the center of each person is the God-given desire to be accepted, forgiven, and loved. Those struggling for identity will appreciate *Prone to Love* as a key to unlock and accept their true hidden self. Enjoy!

REV. PAUL JOHANSSON
Chancellor and Chairman of Elim Bible Institute and College

Has anyone told you that your identity and value is not found in your belief system? Or that identity trumps behavior when you miss the mark? Drawing upon a colorful kaleidoscope of personal stories, *Prone to Love* is thoughtful, hilarious, and revelatory. It beckons us to see Christ unconditionally, more fully resident every day, than we may have before.

Through his reflections on his relationships with his children, his thirty-year-old alarm clock, a flat tire when he was broke, a jolt of lightning during a storm, or confessions of things he did as a bad waiter, Jason takes us below the surface of his premise that love trumps need to discover what we each really need, in fact, *only* need, to become more sure in our Father's love. Becoming sure in the Father's love is the life-quest Jason has set himself on. He believes the destiny of each of us is to start and end well.

His wonderful connection to living life through powerful spirituality vacant of religious overtones and his belief that the life we each dream of is found in a greater encounter with our Father in heaven comes through every page. *Prone to Love* is straightforward and disarming, a breath of fresh air! It takes on some of the hard stuff, and does so with honesty and panache. It's clear that Jason has, as he says, "Stood in love's downpour and been speared through with love's great passion." He is utterly confident that the whole purpose for each of us is to know that God is love, His love is always good, and that we exist to become sure. *Prone to Love* carves a path of discovering the beauty and the power of that certainty.

BONNIE CHAVDA

Founder and Pastor of All Nations Church and The Watch of the Lord

PRONE TO ~~WANDER~~ LOVE

JASON CLARK

DESTINY IMAGE® PUBLISHERS, INC.

P.O. Box 310, Shippensburg, PA 17257-0310

"Promoting Inspired Lives."

This book and all other Destiny Image, Revival Press, MercyPlace, Fresh Bread, Destiny Image Fiction, and Treasure House books are available at Christian bookstores and distributors worldwide.

For a U.S. bookstore nearest you, call 1-800-722-6774.

For more information on foreign distributors, call 717-532-3040.

Reach us on the Internet: www.destinyimage.com.

ISBN 13 TP: 978-0-7684-4249-6

ISBN 13 Ebook: 978-0-7684-8456-4

For Worldwide Distribution, Printed in the U.S.A.

1 2 3 4 5 6 7 8 / 18 17 16 15 14

DEDICATION

This book is dedicated to my wife and best friend, Karen, and my kids, Madeleine True, Ethan Wilde, and Eva Blaze—my favorites. Karen, I can't imagine this journey without you. You amaze me. Your love has revealed our Father's love; it's transformed me. Dreaming with you is changing the world. As a bright fella once said, "I'm at your feet."

Madeleine, my "sunshine," you have one of the brightest promises I've ever seen. When people meet you they can't help but shine. You are a worshiper. You revel in His love and reveal His goodness. The Father loves your songs and adores your presence!

Ethan, my "wild man," you are gentle and fierce. Your promise is powerful and will set people free. The world will never be the same because of you. You dream and carry the melody and rhythms of heaven. The Father not only loves you, He is wild about hanging out with you!

Eva, my "bright eyes," your promise is glorious! Your revelation of God's presence is wondrous, beautiful. New words will be created for God's majesty because of your friendship with Him. The Father thinks you're stunning and loves you intensely!

And this book is dedicated to Jeremy and Kathryn Cole: I tell your story everywhere. The sacrifices you made for our family reaches to the heavens…and pulls heaven down. Your surrender and faith are a rich inheritance and legacy that surpasses your wildest imaginings! Thanks for loving us so well. We love you back!

ACKNOWLEDGEMENTS

Thank You, Father. Your love is the best. May this book be a sweet, sweet sound to Your ears...

A book is never written alone. There are always great influencers—the dreamers and revivalists, the pioneers and reformers, those who have prayed and believed and even died a little, so that a story can be captured.

This book was not written alone. Every time I wrote, you were all with me. Karen's stunning wisdom, and Madeleine's, Ethan's, and Eva's measureless wonder; my dad's steady, unruffled faith and my mom's absolute belief; my father- and mother-in-law, J. V. and Cindy, your trust and support have been life-changing; my sisters, Aimee, Megan, and Kathleen, and brothers, Joel, Josiah, Ben, Eric, Aaron, and Bobby; the dreamers, encouragers, collaborators, and giants in the faith who have loved me in every season: you have challenged and inspired, laughed and cried, undergirded and promoted—and I love you all best!

My friends, both new and old, you were with me when I wrote. Thank you for your wisdom and your grace, for your objection and your trust. Your gift of friendship urges me on.

Lowell and Jennifer, and all the McNaneys, your vision and faith have been a catalyst for revival. We love doing life with you! To the

Chambers who radiate His goodness and the Fletchers who expect; to the Gaetas who transform and the Squyres who know love—both beholding and becoming; to the Wests who live and laugh and the Appleyards who move mountains; and to all our Crossroads family: we love you and are so blessed to run with you after the greater works Jesus promised.

Shawn and Brenda Ring, you showed us how to be giants in the faith. May the world be forever changed by our friendship. Joel and Tennille, your radical display of trust and obedience is transformational, and we are honored to call you friends. Jeremy and Kathryn Cole, there is such a powerful beauty to the surrendered life you guys have exhibited. Scott and Charissa Crowder, your friendship and passion for His presence is an eternal encouragement to us. To the Vogens who think higher, the Prins who faithfully seek heavens perspective, the Skinners who live loved, the Turners who believe, the Berkowitzes who revel and reveal, the Harnishes who hope, the Moseleys who transcend, and to Jacob Early who shines, thank you.

Thank you, Jeff and Julie Watson, you have modeled faithfulness and were the heaven-sent introduction to Destiny Image. To Ronda Ranalli, Mykela Krieg, Terri Meckes and everyone at Destiny Image who have been wonderful champions of the Kingdom, it's been a pleasure and honor writing with this house. John Blase, this is the second time we have worked together and it is good! Your writing gift is unmatched and your wisdom is priceless—it's a much better book because of you. To my new prayer-answered editor and wild-at-heart friend, Allen Arnold, your help was timely and so encouraging. And to my brother Joel who is always the surest hand in the early stages and makes writing fun. Joel, the Michael Douglas reference may be the best line in the book. And I want to thank Kathryn Helmers who was a great sounding board early on in this work. And thanks to Mark Batterson for empowering.

To the spiritual fathers who have poured into our lives: My dad, I'm blessed. Bill Johnson, Graham Cooke, Dan Mohler, Richard Oliver, Kris Vallotton, Danny Silk, Dick Grout, and Mahesh and Bonnie Chavda; thank you for living your faith for the world to see.

For the inspiring sounds of momentum: Anthony Skinner, The Veils, Sleeping At Last, Andy Squyres, Phoenix, Jonathan and Melissa Helser, Mumford & Sons, John Mark McMillan, The Killers, Band of a Thousand, U2, Arcade Fire, Josh Baldwin, M83, The Boxer Rebellion, Brian and Jenn Johnson, Imogen Heap, Jacob Early, The National, Bon Iver, Scott Crowder, Among Savages, Bryan and Katie Torwalt, River Church, Tom Odell, and many more: thank you.

And to all you amazing baristas for the sweet magic bean juice, thanks!

I have never written alone and I am so grateful.

CONTENTS

FOREWORD

Growing up in Canada as a boy automatically made you a hockey player. It was in your blood. My friends and I (the poor kids) played on the streets and ponds while the more affluent children played in organized clubs with all the bells and whistles. But pond or rink, we all dreamed of becoming the next Gordy Howe or Bobby Hull.

So growing up in a "Pentecostal revival" as a boy automatically made me a preacher. Church was as exciting as hockey. The deaf hearing, the blind seeing, the lame walking—I saw it with my own eyes. It was amazing, all the promises of God alive in our church. My pastor was my hero and the glossy magazines in my house were filled with pictures of "men of faith and power." As a boy, I knew God's love, and I also knew I wanted to be a preacher. I spent hours standing in front of the mirror preaching up a storm. My dream was to be a revivalist like my pastor and maybe even have my own glossy magazine cover one day.

As a kid, church was every night of the week and the source of some of my best adventures. Over my past sixty-three years, I have adventured in the church deep and wide—charismatic, Baptist, Methodist, nondenominational—the persuasions and movements have all added to my story.

I've tasted and seen that the Lord is good. And I love the church—the bride of Christ. But over the years, the wide-eyed dreams of a boy were beaten and bloodied in the trenches of the church. Over the years, my passion was muddied as I experienced the carnage and cannibalism of power-hungry men who dreamed of having their own magazine some day. Church disappointed me. I became disillusioned with her.

Equally disappointing was that I became disillusioned with myself as well. I was convinced that I too was flawed. I would never be truly trustworthy and thus would never see the power of God flowing through my fingertips. And somewhere along the way I accidentally swore off on ever being a revivalist.

As I grew older, the lie was reinforced by my own failures. I was not trustworthy and worse, I was unlovely and unworthy. Who was I to be cynical with the church when my own life looked nothing like the promises of my youth? I became more and more reluctant to risk. My dreams of the church, a beautiful bride, were fading and I began to settle for the routine, the mundane, and the safe.

I have since learned that a lie is the only thing that can remove us from our promise, the only thing that can separate us from the tangible experience of a revived life. The only power Satan has is the power of the lie. The enemy of our souls only purpose is to conceal, distort, and destroy our true identity. He wants us to believe that we are untrustworthy, unlovely, and unworthy.

But His light has come! And light changes everything! Because of the cross, the lie no longer has a voice—unless I decide to give it one. In the last several years, I have discovered that my promise, the true dream of my youth, wasn't a glossy magazine or the title of pastor. It wasn't even the power of His presence or revival. My promise is simple—to know He loves me and is entirely captivated by my loveliness. And I have become so filled with anticipation that I can't wait till morning. I am in the biggest learning curve of my life! He loves me!

It gets sweeter as the days go by,
It gets sweeter as the moments fly.
His love is richer, deeper, fuller, sweeter,
Sweeter, sweeter, sweeter as the days goes by.[1]

I sang this as a boy, and it's truer still!

I am learning that "He loves me" isn't just an introduction or even a chapter in our story; it's the book. And every new chapter is a spin-off of this one central revelation. From creation to the cross, and from the cross onward, "He loves me" is the center and focal point of both this life and the life to come. His love for me is what gives me value, it's what makes me trustworthy and lovely.

I think heaven will be an eternity of "ahs and ahas" of amazement at how deep, how wide, and how high His love really is—beautiful vistas at every new bend in the road. But what I am coming to learn is that we don't have to wait! We can know this love and live heaven here and now!

Since the days when the fullest revelation of Love walked the earth in the form of a man, light has continued to dawn. As Jesus was leaving the earth, those closest to Him were in the biggest learning curve of their lives. And at the end of John's apostolic journey, he was still in amazement at how much better and bigger God actually was.

John and the apostles were "getting it" in increasing measures as their capacity for "getting it" increased.

Earth may still seem a long way from heaven. But Jesus's prayer in Matthew 6 was that earth would be transformed in the light of heaven. And this is the story of heaven, this is heaven's song, "We are loved."

Occasionally someone comes along who puts things into words that expose the lies and cause my heart to pitter-patter. My mind may be struggling to grasp what is going on while my heart is burning within me, for it is with the heart, not the head, that we "get it." And Jason is "getting it!"

As Jason's parents, we've had front row seats in his story. Mary and I get to watch up close. We have actually been strapped to the front of this transformation, watching the gory turn into glory, and we get to declare, although the ride is far from over and nothing short of delightful, that our hearts are burning within us!

He loves me! Jason has been living with a reckless abandon and discovering our truly good Father along the way. In this book, Jason is bringing hidden things to light, exposing lies that have kept us in bondage, and offering us more tools for transformation. And as he puts truths into stories I can understand and relate with, I find myself overwhelmed again and again at how much bigger and how much better my Father is. I never imagined He would be this accessible and good—really good.

Prone to Love is filled with fresh insights where you will discover you are as near to Him right now as you will ever be, and that access to everything He is has already been granted.

God willing, over the next forty years or so that Mary and I will still be on this side of eternity, we are living with joyful anticipation as we dream, explore, and continue to discover the deep love of our Father. And His love will continue to dawn in the lives of our grandkids and great-grandkids as they expound on and expand the truths of what was won for us at Calvary. He loves us!

I love the church and I see something fresh and beautiful on the horizon. And I find myself running after it with reckless abandon, willing to believe once more for brighter, better, and bolder expressions in His beautiful bride.

LLOYD CLARK

Note

1.   "Sweeter as the Days Go By," written by Frank Edward and Gordon Wilson. 2Lyrics © EMI Music Publishing, Universal Music Publishing Group, Sony/ATV Music Publishing, LLC.

PROLOGUE

I met a philosophy professor the other day. Well, actually I see him a few times a week. He frequents the same coffee shop as me. We have often caught each other's eye over our laptops from across the room. It was just a matter of time before we struck up a conversation. He is a nice man and very smart, just like me. He is also writing a book and enjoys the coffee shop atmosphere, just like me.

I asked him what his book was about one day. He spoke for a couple minutes about other philosophers, comparing his thought with theirs. I recognized a few of the names and remember hearing something about "mother issues," but I was definitely in over my head. I think he saw it on my face, so he said, "Really, I am writing about the human condition."

He then began to explain the state of mankind in such abstract terms that I was soon lost again—"which is good if you are a philosophy professor," I thought. By the time he was finished talking, as best as I could tell, his book seemed to be about nothing. At first I was impressed because I'm pretty sure writing a book about nothing is a lot harder than writing about something. And also, who doesn't love Seinfeld?

While I was trying to form a question that didn't embarrass either of us, he continued, "What is pain? What is joy, or love?" he asked. "They are just feelings, just needs—life is a random roll of the dice.

Nothing in this universe is sure; everything is determined by what you feel and by what you need."

"It really is a book about nothing," I thought again to myself. And I also thought about how funny Kramer looks when he bursts through Seinfeld's door. Yeah, I was multitasking.

He went on to say that man is the sum of what we feel, the sum of our needs—emotionally and physically. There is no great purpose or meaning to life, and all our philosophies and theologies are simply the wild imaginings of men who need to feel a sense of purpose. In the end, life is about gratifying our senses while trying to avoid pain. Life is one big need-driven experience he claimed.

Sometimes my mouth opens and my vocal chords push words out before my head can get involved. It can be very embarrassing, like when I confused the words *Neapolitan* and *menopause*. (No wait, it was my sister Aimee who did that.)

Oh, like when I was eating spicy chicken curry and thanked God that the Native Americans came up with this genius food. (No, it was my brother Joel that time.)

Oh yeah, like the time I thought Sonny Bono and Bono were the same person and wondered how that worked with Cher. (Nope, that wasn't me either; it was the girl I fell head over heals in love with and married.)

Oh, now I remember. There was the time I said to a philosophy professor who was writing a book, "So you are writing a book about nothing?"

He smiled. It was a tired smile. He didn't seem to notice my embarrassment at my outburst or consider my question odd. In fact, I think he was very familiar with this question. "In a way, yes," he replied.

I was at a loss for words. I couldn't think of anything else to say about his book. I almost mentioned Seinfeld to make him feel better.

"That show was about nothing and seemed to work," I thought. But this time I was able to control my vocal chords.

It was overwhelming, the idea of writing a book about nothing. Our only common denominator was that both of us were writing books. But after that our two roads diverged. My sincerest prayer is that my book would be about something—and not just *any* something.

I finally asked, "So how long have you been working on your book?"

"For almost twenty years."

Twenty years! That broke my heart. That a man would write faithfully for twenty years is amazing. That a man can write about nothing for twenty years is excruciating. I felt sad for this tired man who seemed to have been searching for some truth in a universe where he is convinced truth doesn't exist.

I couldn't take it anymore. So I asked him the question that should never be asked of a philosophy professor: "Where does God fit in?"

I watched him physically shift into professor mode. He was both quick to acknowledge that religion plays a role in philosophy but also that religion was for weak-minded individuals.

"Good thing I didn't tell him what I was writing about," I thought.

But I hadn't asked him about religion, I'd asked about God. He had done what many often do and confused the two as being one and the same. So I tried the same question from a different angle.

"Where does Love fit in?"

He looked at me—the look was one of absolute exhaustion, as if this question was just too much for him. "Love is a subjective feeling, a physiological need," he responded.

"But what if you're wrong? What if it isn't?" I asked. "What if Love is the very foundation of everything? What if Love is the beginning and the end and everything in between and everything after? What if Love answers every question that aches in the heart of humanity? What if Love is more than a feeling? What if Love meets every need?"

He looked at me, annoyed. I think this question is the one that he found embarrassing, as if I had just taken leave of my senses. My heart broke. I could see this man had been wounded deeply at some point in his life. He clearly no longer believed in Love.

Then I sensed his dismissal, our conversation coming to a close. But I wanted to ask him so many more questions. I wanted to ask him questions that if answered in Spirit and Truth would radically forever change the way this professor thinks.

What if Love created everything? What if Love saw what He had created and said, "It is good"?—which is something Love would probably say. What if Love has all authority but does not control? What if Love is about freedom? What if Love walked the earth as a man, died, and rose again so that we could be set free, free to fully receive love and to love in return? What if Love isn't a feeling but a tangible expression of that same freedom? What if Love had the power to meet every need that ever existed?

These thoughts burst in my heart.

Love! It's a profoundly infinite and beautiful Person, a measureless revelation. Love is the best discovery, the only story worth writing about.

Another writer once put it this way: *"If every one of* (the things Love did) *were written down, I suppose that even the whole world would not have room for the books that would be written"* (John 21:25).

If only my new philosophy professor friend knew this Love, well, then he could know what it is to live and write with purpose and destiny and legacy. He could spend the next twenty years filling the world with books about something.

Before he packed up to go, he asked what I was writing about. I told him that I was writing a book about Love. I said, "It's going to be something."

He said he would like to read it sometime.

Chapter One

I DON'T WANT TO BE DESPERATE FOR GOD

A Dysfunctional Relationship

I wish I'd been at the table, but I wasn't. But two of my hero friends were—Kris Vallotton and Graham Cooke. Both are incredible men of God who have greatly influenced my life. As Kris tells the story, both he and Graham were at a dinner with several other leaders. The food was good, the conversation even better. While everyone else at the table was in lively discussion, Graham was eating quietly. Suddenly, halfway through his dinner, Graham blurted out, "I don't want to be desperate for God!" Then he went back to eating.

The once lively table was now quiet. Everyone was waiting for Graham to elaborate, but he had returned to his meal. Kris began to digest Graham's outburst. It didn't appear relevant to his last conversation, nor any of the others throughout the night. Finally, Kris broke the confused silence. "Graham, what do you mean?"

What Graham said next radically changed my life, the aha moment in a journey thirty-six years in the making. And, in fact, the hope of conveying it to you is the reason I've written this book. Graham said, "A relationship where the son is always desperate for the Father is dysfunctional."

The Crier

I've sent a fire to burn inside your soul.[1]

I was twenty-two and newly married to my dazzling wife, Karen. I went with dazzling here as she doesn't like it when I call her "my lovely wife." Apparently, lovely is for grandmas and fine china. But she is lovely, and in a dazzling way, like a sudden breath of crisp fall air, or a thrilling stolen kiss in her parents' kitchen, which is way better than grandmas or fine china.

I was finishing up at Elim, a Bible college that had an amazing tradition of praying for the graduating students. They actually devoted a whole week to it. Students and faculty would meet in the chapel several hours each day and pray corporately while a few elders in the faith—who were led by the Holy Spirit—would give specific words of encouragement and direction to the graduates.

Two chairs were set in the front of the auditorium. Karen sat with me in what students had nicknamed "the hot seats." The elders gathered around us as loving fathers and mothers. Sylvia Evans, a woman in her fifties, who lived boldly for God on the mission field abroad and in the U.S., stepped near. Very kindly she said, "Jason." She paused, looking me in the eyes until she knew she had my full attention. "Jason, I feel like God is saying that you see yourself as a spiritual dwarf. But He wants you to know that He sees you as a spiritual giant."

I began to cry.

Yeah, I'm a crier. I can be moved to tears. Like when I recently found the brown paper bag in our minivan with an apple, a granola bar, a small package of pretzels, and a note inside. The note was written in the hand of my stunning eleven-year-old daughter, Madeleine, and it accompanied the bagged lunch she had prepared for the men and women we so often see standing with a sign at the stoplight. The note read, "Dear loved one, Jesus loves you and I want you to have this food." Yeah, there were tears.

But usually my tears are controlled. However, when Sylvia spoke the heart of God over me, I didn't just shed a few tears, I sobbed—the kind where you need a box of tissues. I think the biblical word is *wept*; it makes those witnessing uncomfortable, they want and almost need to look away. But I couldn't help it; I couldn't contain myself. The idea that God saw me as a spiritual giant, well, it seemed too good to be true. And yet everything in me longed to believe it!

I don't know about you, but I have lived most of my life from that dwarf's perspective.

Looking back now, I know why Sylvia's statement, which came directly from heaven, so messed me up. For just a moment, I saw myself from my heavenly Father's perspective. I was completely unprepared for what I saw—I couldn't even function. It was contrary to what I believed yet so wonderfully good that I was overwhelmed. In that moment, God's perspective exposed and gave resolve to my ferocious internal battle. A battle I had been born into, a battle regarding my identity. A battle I am still engaged in, and I'm pretty sure I'm not the only one.

Starving

I was in the living room last night, sitting on the couch working on my laptop, and in comes Ethan. The stereo was cranked with Brian and Jenn Johnson singing the beautiful hymn "Here Is Love." The lyrics melt me every time I hear them:

> Here is love, vast as the ocean,
> Loving kindness as the flood...[2]

Ethan yelled over the music. It took me a moment to figure out what he wanted. It shouldn't have, it's almost always one of three things: XBOX, permission to go down the street to his friend's house, or food. I turned the music down just in time to hear him proclaim that he was "starving, Dad!" He's always starving.

I looked at him in mock confusion. "Starving? Again? Didn't you just have a banana, some chips, and a granola bar like half an hour ago?"

I have often given Ethan the definition of starving: "To die or perish from lack of food or nourishment."[3] When finished defining the word, we will both agree he isn't actually starving; he's just hungry, or more likely, bored. However, my son's memory seems to be flawed as often, later in the same day, he will forget the definition of the word and use it incorrectly again.

I could hear Brian singing in the background:

Grace and love, like mighty rivers,
Poured incessant from above...

Ethan has never been "starving." We are so blessed! Ethan could never truly use words like *starving*, or *desperate*, or even a simple word like *need*. Ethan has never truly *needed* food.

And then he asked an awesome question: "So Dad, what's for dinner?"

That's a *good* question, a very telling question regarding our relationship. First, Ethan expects to eat. Second, he acknowledges that it is both my role to feed him and to help him decide what he eats. Ethan's question reveals that he and I are in a healthy father-son relationship.

I am a good father. I tell my kids all the time and they believe me. But as amazing a father as I am, I don't hold a candle, or a firebrand, or any other source of light, to my heavenly Father. He's the *cat's meow...* yeah, I'm bringing it back.

The Perfect Father

I pledge my head to a holy love.

When I first heard Graham Cooke's statement, "I don't want to be desperate for God," I knew it was big. I knew it was life-changing big. His statement reverberated in my heart like a thunderclap and I was convinced to my core that it was a profound truth just for me, but maybe for you as well.

I have been telling God about my needs for my entire life. Need has been a part of our relational DNA; it's a familiar theme, a comfortable reality, our love language. When I wake, throughout my day, and before I sleep, I talk with God often from the perspective of my needs or the needs of my family and friends. And I often use the same words Ethan uses. Words like *starving* and *desperate* are commonplace adjectives for my interaction with God.

For weeks I contemplated Graham's outburst. I could sense God had a beautiful revelation for me in those words. Every time I thought about it, I asked God to reveal His heart to me. Then one day, in the middle of a run, God asked me a question.

I like to run, and when I run I feel His pleasure (sorry). But it's true, in that running has become a sweet God-time for me—we have many deep conversations. I run approximately five times a week, about three miles each outing. You could say I am a running hero! You could say that if you wanted to.

I called myself a running hero when I first started running. Then I met real runners, those who kept track of their time and their heart rate. Oh, and apparently "real runners"—they run five miles before breakfast. Real runners pass me like I'm standing still, halfway through their ten-mile, relaxed, mid-week jaunt. But I still like to call myself a running hero.

So I was out for a run when God started speaking to my heart. "Jason, remember that word given to you fifteen years ago from Sylvia

Evans? I told you I see you as a spiritual giant. Well, I have been saying it to you every day since. I haven't changed My mind and I never will."

Then God said something profound, which God is prone to do. "Jason, it's illegal for you to entertain feelings of insecurity."

As I ran, I began to cry—yes, again. God continued, "Either agree with Me or call Me a liar. There are no longer any other options for you."

If it sounds a little strong, it's because it was, but in a stunningly perfect way!

Before I could even begin to digest all God was speaking into my heart, He asked me another very profound question. A question that at first seemed disconnected to His previous statements.

"Jason, am I a perfect Father?"

"Yes," I said. I did actually say it.

God continued speaking to my heart. "If I am a perfect Father and we are in a dysfunctional relationship, then it's not on Me."

That statement from God wasn't a question; it was revelation. It was an invitation to know God in a way I never had before. It hit me so hard I had to stop running (which I didn't actually mind); I was kind of out of breath from the crying. God's statement answered the question that had been resounding in my heart since I had first heard Graham Cooke's comment.

After about a half mile of walking and reveling in this new thought, I spoke out loud to God a declaration both beautiful and dangerous: "Father, I will no longer allow our relationship to be determined by my need."

Need < Love

I don't know if you have ever thought about it like this, but *need* is what defines life here on planet earth. In fact, time itself is the father of need. The universe was created as finite, meaning there is a beginning and an end. In a finite reality, need is the principle in which time exists, it's the skeleton upon which reality hangs.

Need is the final singular truth by which our world operates. Humanity exists inside the confines of need. We trade in the currency of need. It is the foundational structure of our DNA. It's the defining core value of our very existence. You could say that we are slaves to need.

Need is with us when we wake and when we sleep. And it's not an abstract idea. It's probably the most real thing many of us know. It's an absolute, a physical, emotional, and spiritual reality woven into the very fabric of our existence.

For instance, we need air to breathe and we need gravity to keep us from floating away. We need food to sustain our bodies. We need clothes and shelter. We need money to buy clothes and shelter. We need jobs to make money so we can buy clothes and shelter. We need a good economy to provide jobs.

What I am trying to communicate is that we are one big walking, talking, breathing, need.

It's not a bad thing. It's actually beautifully brilliant if seen from God's perspective. He created it. And because God is good, He only has good ideas and only creates good things. I believe God created need for one reason: to reveal His love. But I'm getting a little ahead of myself.

So creation took its first breath in the wonderful certainty of need. Our heavenly Father created a finite reality in which men and women dwell. And then He did something odd and absolutely amazing, He breathed His Spirit, His *Neuma* into us. He put eternal spirits in finite bodies. He introduced the immeasurable into a world controlled by measurements. He made humankind in His image—Love.

God is love and He is always good. It says so in my Bible. And yours too.

Love is the beginning and the end, and everything in between, and everything before and everything after. Love is infinite, immeasurable.

Love is complete. Love is the answer, not the question. Love is always good. That's all in the Book as well.

Now here's my crazy thought. While need is the very substance of our existence, it has no place in God's reality. And if God is love, then you could say it like this: need cannot exist in love. Need is actually counter to the nature of love. Love trumps every need, every time. It's the good news that only gets better.

I would like to suggest that need fosters insecurity, while love cultivates identity. Stick with me, I think I'm on to something big here. I believe there is a revelation of love available to every one of us that settles the insecurity of need, that sets us free to become sons and daughters of a perfectly good, perfectly loving, heavenly Father.

Before Jesus's resurrection, we lived in a world where every emotion, every decision, and every moment was defined by need, by what we didn't have and needed or what we would need later on.

After Jesus's resurrection, our heavenly Father invited humanity to live free of the controls of need in a glorious infinite revelation—Love. The core value of our very existence was redeemed from a need-based reality to an intimate, measureless love relationship.

Jesus came and revealed the Father. He took all of our needs upon Himself and died. He took a need-based existence to the grave where it always belonged. And upon His resurrection, He introduced us to a greater revelation of intimacy with our heavenly Father, and access to the infinite reality of His Kingdom of love—heaven on earth.

Papa

Went to see the northern light,
So bright, reflected in Your eyes.

After Papa died that first time, he was a better man—full of joy and grace and love.

My papa was a minister. He was a good man before he died. He was also a flawed man who hadn't fully encountered his heavenly Father's love. Before he died, he was a happy man, but his joy was incomplete as it was suffocated by the uncertainty of need. Before he died, Papa was an accomplished man. He was also insecure in his ministry, constantly moving and starting over, never quite comfortable in his own skin. He did some amazing things before he died; he also inflicted some very large wounds.

But the best was meant for last. God, in His measureless goodness, gave Papa revelation and more time.

Papa woke up and the first thing he saw was a calendar and a clock—sad reminders of an inferior reality. He was in a hospital bed and the way he told it, everything hurt. He had three broken ribs, which he had sustained during CPR performed on him by his son. He had been at a family reunion celebration. Papa had just entered the car when he felt severe chest pain. He collapsed in the back seat and was pulled from the car. And that's where he died that first time.

Papa visited us six months after he died. He and Nana stayed with our family, out in the beautiful Pacific Northwest, for a whole week. It was an amazing time. A time where my parents and my grandparents laughed together like I'd never seen before. Mom and Dad have told me since that there were tears too, as Papa shared his heart and asked forgiveness for past wrongs.

During the week they were with us, we had a rare snowstorm. This kept us all indoors. Papa and Nana had discovered a new fantastic game—Skip-Bo—which they introduced to us. We sat around the kitchen table every night and played for hours. We laughed and told stories. The best story was the one Papa shared, about when he died and went to heaven and met Jesus face to face.

After collapsing in the car, he found himself in heaven surrounded by angels and a "cloud of glory." He said that the "rejoicing and happiness was indescribable." There were other people with him. He talked with and recognized every one of them. They were the closest of family even though they all had just met. He said the light in heaven is beautiful, almost alive—it wasn't from the sun and it was everywhere.

Suddenly he was greeted by the King of kings! Jesus was stunning, absolutely glorious! He was standing, radiant in light, holding a scroll. He was reading it to Himself, unscrolling and smiling as He read. Then He looked at Papa and said, "This is really good!"

Papa laughed and then asked, "What are You reading?"

Jesus responded, "Your book. I want You to finish it!"

So Papa woke up in a hospital bed to a clock and a calendar that measures time, illuminated by artificial light. For a moment he was overcome with sadness.

He later wrote, "In my hospital room I felt I was between heaven and earth and tended to resent both the calendar and the clock. I learned that heaven is altogether perfect. Nothing is more perfect than the perfection I saw there."

However, it wasn't long before he was smiling and laughing once again. It was the kind of smiling and laughing that just compelled those around him to join in. You see, he had stood face to face with Jesus, he had seen and experienced heaven, he was confident in love. He was transformed. He was a better man.

At home one afternoon, about six months after their visit, Papa found Nana sitting with their daughter, my Aunt Joy, around the kitchen table. "I have completed the final proofread for the editor," he said. Then he grinned, "My book is finished."

Papa left the kitchen to take a short nap before the celebration dinner they had planned for later that evening. He fell asleep and went to heaven that night for the second and final time, the very same day he finished his book.

My papa wrote in his book about how love changes us. "His love can totally revolutionize our thinking about ourselves. When we live in His love, we do not labor to love."[4]

He also wrote about how living heaven on earth is the calling of every believer:

> We were meant for heaven and heaven was meant for us…
> joy for the Christian comes when we live in heavenly grace.
> The reality of heaven must already be our experience on
> earth. The Christian faith thinks miraculously.[5]

My papa experienced a small taste of heaven—literally. He came back to earth a transformed man. He righted past wrongs and loved in a way he never had before. He became sure, secure in God's love, and he brought a little bit of heaven back with him.

For me, looking back on my papa's story, I am beginning to think that while earth trades in the commodity of need, heaven operates in the revelation of love. I think that's why Jesus actually taught us to pray, "Thy Kingdom come on earth as it is in heaven" (see Matt. 6:10). He knew that Love was the answer to every need.

I believe we live in two realities, one greater than the other. The first is the one of which we are often the most aware. In this reality we know words like *starving* or *desperate*, we live in the ache of insecurity—*need* defines everything. But I am coming into a conviction that there is a greater reality, a greater revelation available to us where the words describing need are forever settled.

Let's Go Find this Kingdom Come

Come on in out of the cold, come home.

If you think about it, Love walked the earth in the body of Jesus. And while Jesus very much lived *on* earth, He very much lived *from* heaven. So everywhere Love went, heaven invaded earth. What's astounding to me is that every need that was presented to Love was met and fully answered—physically, emotionally, and spiritually—through the power of heaven. And it often looked miraculous.

Love healed the sick, fed the hungry, and raised the dead. Love trumped every need, every time. Love forgave the prostitute, the adulterer, the thief, and the liar. Again, Love trumped every need, every time. Love fed the hungry, paid taxes, calmed the storm, and turned water into wine. Again, every time Love trumped.

I believe the Kingdom of heaven operates from a different core value than earth. While earth revolves around the reality of need, heaven exists in the revelation of love. Everything in the Kingdom of heaven operates, hinges, and moves in that reality. Love trumps.

Need doesn't exist in heaven. We won't need to be healed in heaven; there is no sickness there. We won't need to feel loved; we will know and become love. We won't know poverty, sadness, or confusion; our Father is rich in mercy and grace. We won't have any questions about why we exist; the manifest glory of God will make it clear.

As a good friend of mine, Andy Squyres, says, "Earth is the only place we can love God while in need." We have the incredible opportunity to discover that even while need is very much a part of our lives, love always trumps. Isn't that amazing? It's such an eternal heavenly perspective! There is no need in heaven.

I believe all of heaven is available now—all of it. We have access to the same heaven Jesus did. He revealed that we could live in the same revelation of our Father that He lived in when He taught us to pray, "Thy Kingdom come on earth as it is in heaven" (see Matt. 6:10). We can love in the same powerful, miraculous, heaven-to-earth way Jesus loved.

Jesus told us that the Kingdom of heaven, the place that operates in love, is at hand. Essentially, this Kingdom is within reach. I am convinced we are here to discover it in every area of our lives.

Let's go find this Kingdom come.

The Lord's Prayer

This, then, is how you should pray: "Our Father in heaven, hallowed be Your name, Your kingdom come, Your will be done on earth as it is in heaven. Give us today our daily bread" (Matthew 6:9-11).

Jesus taught us how to pray about need. *"Give us this day our daily bread."* The fact is that we have a good Father who wants us to come to Him with our needs.

But before daily bread, Jesus said we are to pray, *"Your kingdom come…on earth as it is in heaven."*

If *"on earth as it is in heaven"* comes before *"daily bread,"* then our need is in right relationship with our revelation and we never have to pray desperate prayers. If *"on earth as it is in heaven"* comes before *"daily bread,"* our relationship with God will never be dysfunctional.

Every Need, Every Time

This love, this revival, it's shaking the ground,
All of this glory a deafening sound.

He is love when I am insecure or when I see myself as a spiritual dwarf. He is love when I am in pain; He is love when I am disillusioned, when I am unsure. He is love when I'm afraid or anxious. He is love when I am confused or distressed or dying. And love is good, always.

Love is good when I feel forgotten or insignificant, when I am insecure. Love answers those needs.

Love is good when there isn't enough food; when there is an earthquake or a tornado or tsunami. Love answers those needs.

Love is good when there is sickness or poverty or abuse or hate. Love answers those needs.

Love is always good and love is always the answer. It's the answer to every question my heart is asking. Love is sure and confident and gentle and kind and bold. Love answers all my emotional, physical, and spiritual questions. Love trumps every need—every time.

A Greater Revelation

Let me find my joy complete,
Let me see, oh love, be my sweet witness.

Don't get me wrong. I have physical, emotional, and spiritual needs that assault me from the moment I wake up to the moment I go back to sleep, and sometimes they follow me into my dreams. But I am coming into a beautiful understanding that all my needs are answered in a greater revelation of His love and therefore I must experience more!

I am becoming convinced that the Christian life is not meant to revolve around need, but is instead a headlong daring discovery of His love. I am convinced that my relationship with my heavenly Father is meant to be just like the one Jesus had with His—a relationship defined by love and trust, a relationship with a perfect, always good Father who releases me into the sureness of my identity as His son.

I think it is actually possible to live on earth, this place that revolves around need and births insecurity, in a way where I am not confined or restricted or enslaved to need. I am becoming sure in His love.

You see, I have become a son of an infinitely good and loving Father with all of heaven at my beck and call.

Spiritual Giants

And Your glory descends,
Hey friends, it's time we got going.

Do you remember Sylvia Evans's words to me as I graduated? I would like to suggest that God sees every one of us as spiritual giants! Seriously. That's how He sees you. He has felt that way about you since the beginning of time. He has been telling you about it since you took your first breath. You heard Him loud and clear the moment you said yes to Him, yes to the finished work of Jesus's death and resurrection. He hasn't changed His mind since and He never will.

I would also like to suggest that you have one of two options: either agree with Him and leap into His love, or don't believe Him and keep battling that overwhelming insecurity. Either jump head first into the measureless expanse of His love or continue to be dwarfed by this world's preoccupation with need.

This book is an invitation to begin to step away from the dysfunction of need and into the freedom, authority, and power of love. We're not starving. His love is what we live in and move in and have our being in. It's all there. We just have to trust it. We simply have to trust that love trumps.

Notes

1. Unless otherwise noted, all the lyrics in this book are from Jason Clark's songs. The songs span several albums and singles including *Surrendered and Untamed* and his forthcoming EP entitled *Heaven's Crush*.

2. This version of "Here Is Love" is sung by Brian and Jenn Johnson on their album, *Love Came Down*.

3. "Starving," from *Dictionary.com*, http://dictionary.reference.com/browse/starving?s=t, accessed July 16, 2013.

4.   D. L. Niswander, *Christians Face the New Age* (Welch Publishing Company Inc., 1989).

5.   Ibid.

Chapter Two

A GOOD STORM

The Lake, Part One

I was disoriented. It felt like I'd been speared through to my heart.

We were standing chest deep in the lake under an elevated dock. I was dazed. Someone was laughing. It took me a second to realize it was myself. I watched as my brother Joel's face shifted from bewildered to terror. Eyes wide, he screamed, "Get out of the water!" I was having a hard time understanding what was going on, my ears were ringing and my head was cloudy, but his instructions seemed right. We needed to get out of the water...

My Theology

This is love! This is love, and I can't let go!

I love to write in coffee shops—the laid-back atmosphere, people meeting other people, most of the time happily. I also happen to be a fan of coffee. I'm not sure who first discovered it, and I refuse to Google it. Some things are better left to the imagination. If I Google it, then my theory regarding the coffee bean and how it was originally considered to have magical powers would have to be abandoned.

And then I couldn't say, "I'm drinking magic bean juice," which I say sometimes.

We may have never met, but you know me. I'm the guy in the corner of Starbucks with the oversized noise-cancelling headphones, the MacBook—because all good writers use Macs—and The North Face laptop bag (a gift from a friend way cooler than me). On the best days, the music becomes my momentum and God's presence my catalyst. On the worst days, the magic bean juice does the trick.

I love getting to know the baristas and the other regulars that frequent the shop. Over time you develop friendships. Some of my closest friends started out as coffee shop friends. Recently, I got talking with a regular. Through previous conversations, I've pieced a bit of his life together.

He is a tough fella, in his sixties. He had grown up as a rancher in the Midwest. He had been a minister "in a past life." He had lost his wife and had a few grown kids scattered across the U.S. He loved God, but best I could tell, somewhere along his journey some of God's people had hurt him. He didn't have much use for the church anymore. He could find passion when he talked about church, but it was usually when he was pointing out its hypocrisies and failures.

This fella reads a lot of history, but theology is his favorite—any theology, any religion. He sits for hours in the coffee shop reading some old book, always thicker than the last, and never any titles I know. But once he found out I was a "Christian writer," his new favorite hobby was to challenge me with sweeping questions about theology. He loves to talk about Scripture. Every nuance is intriguing, every word is a question, and every mystery is waiting to be discussed, if not debated. I learned rather quickly that it's not a good idea to ask him what he was reading unless I had some free time.

I'm not, by the way, a "Christian writer." I'm just a guy who writes about Love. I am not much of a theologian either, or at least I'm not a proper theologian. You know, the kind of person that loves theology religiously. Come to think of it, I'm not very religious at all. In fact, I can't stand most things about religion.

I do have a core theology though. It's quite simple: God is love and He is always good. It's my position on everything. And I'm not much into debating it. I'd rather show than tell.

"How's your day going?" my sixtyish coffee shop friend asked me.

Before I had fully removed my headphones, he had launched into the book he was currently reading. I can't remember what it was called. The Veils was still playing when he gave the title. I paused my iTunes.

He started quoting Scriptures faster than I could Google them and pointing out the hypocrisies of certain Christian leaders, most of whom I had never heard.

"He's fired up!" I thought.

I once heard a hero friend of mine, Bill Johnson, say that he believes "Jesus is perfect theology." I like that…a lot. So I don't want you to mis-understand me when I say I'm not a proper theologian, it's just that I'm only interested in the theology Bill described.

So while this guy hurtled Scriptures, I tried to keep up. But it soon became apparent that I couldn't play ball with this fella. As I listened to him, I began to pray in my heart, "Father, how do You see this man? What are You saying right now?" Immediately, I felt God's presence—His love. Suddenly I was overwhelmed with love for the guy who was mid-sermon.

The question I'd asked God was so beautifully answered by His presence that I abruptly interrupted him to ask the same question, "What is God saying to you right now?"

He paused for a moment. This question seemed out of place. Ironic? Yeah, a little.

"I'm sorry?" he asked.

"What is God saying right at this moment, to you?" I asked again. I wasn't being difficult or clever. We weren't in a competition for significance, I wasn't trying to win an argument, and I don't need to be right. I know that seems like an odd statement from a man who writes books, but it's a freedom I've been growing in for years. Don't get me wrong, I like to be right, I just don't *need* to be.

When the Holy Spirit answered my question, I felt I had the answer to the question that's ached inside the heart of my coffee shop friend for years.

He finally got his head around the question and began to reference the Scripture and the leader he'd just finished raking over the coals, but I interrupted him to ask again, "What is He saying to you *right now*, in this instant?"

He seemed distressed by the question.

It's not really a distressing question unless you aren't sure of the answer.

I continued, "God just told me He is madly in love with you. He particularly loves your mind and He is also immensely proud of you—especially regarding how you raised your kids."

It was that simple, it was that beautiful. Love always is.

For a moment my rugged sixty-something coffee shop friend looked like he had just been speared to the heart, then there were tears. He smiled, his eyes alive in a way I had not seen before. He caught his breath, then again. I could see he was trying to maintain the appearance of control. Then shakily he whispered, "Thank you."

It's amazing how even the smallest glimpse of our Father's love, the slightest brush with His presence, can transform. The moment I shared that short but sweet message from our heavenly Father, our conversation radically shifted. I got to tell him about my theology, which I've mentioned but let me repeat it: God is love. His love is always good. And we exist to become sure of that love.

We had a beautiful time of fellowship as we discussed in Spirit and Truth the nature of God's always-good love.

The Lake, Part Two

I was five and my cousin Mark was six. One minute it was a sunny afternoon, and the next the wind began to howl and dark clouds rolled in. We sat in my blue kiddie pool watching in amazement as the sky began to flash and the thunder roar. It was a surprise thunderstorm, both powerful and dangerous. Mark and I got out of the water and did what any clever five- and six-year-old would do. We marched and we sang:

> *It's raining, it's pouring.*
> *The old man is snoring.*

Midway through our hymn, the sky was torn as a brilliant white lightning bolt streaked down, exploding at the end of the driveway. We stopped marching, mouths open, eyes wide. And then I laughed. It was a natural response to the magic we had just experienced. It was wholly unexplainable and absolutely glorious.

Once again we sang, this time raucously at the top of our lungs:

> *Bumped his head and he went to bed,*
> *And he couldn't get up in the morning.*

We stomped, almost dancing in circles, around the circumference of my little blue plastic pool. It's a memory I'll never forget, only slightly dampened by the arrival of my mother's shrill, anxious, blood-curdling screams.

"Jason! Mark! Come inside! Now!" She seemed as possessed as I felt. She gestured hysterically for us to hurry to the porch. By the time Mark and I stood in the kitchen, wrapped in towels and dripping water on the linoleum, I had, if not a clear understanding, at least a grasp of what happens when a little boy gets struck by lightning.

Some children, after hearing about blackened toenails and smoking heads, would never go out in a thunderstorm again. But it was too late for me. I experienced, if only for a moment, the glorious wonder of standing in a downpour.

So the other day, while out jet skiing with my brothers Ben, Joel, and Josiah, I couldn't help but feel intoxicated by the storm.

It came up while Joel, Ben, and I were on the open water. We killed the engines to the jet skis. The lake was eerily calm and empty of all boaters, except us. There was no wind; the only sound was the gentle movement of water. In minutes the sky had changed from bright afternoon to dusk. We watched as sheets of rain hit the far end of the lake, a great wall of darkness advancing toward us. It was violent and beautiful. Then the lightning began to strike and we started our counting—just like when we were kids! "One, one thousand, two, one thousand…" The thunder rumbled. "Two miles away," Joel said, laughing. Ben was wide-eyed and I was grinning.

Another flash, "One, one thousand—" BOOM! It crashed over our heads. My mother's voice faintly tugged at my mind. "Maybe we should start for shore?" I suggested.

"Yeah," Ben agreed. He was in the water but had started climbing onto the back of Joel's jet ski.

CRACK, BOOM! "That one was close," I yelled over a sudden gust of wind. I was smiling. I couldn't help it. But we could all hear Mom's voice now. We raced for shore.

Josiah had been waiting for us in the water near the pier. "Cutting it close!" he said, laughing nervously. He helped us dock the skis just as the great wall of violence found us. It was amazing. Nature at its fiercest is magnificent to behold. We were fascinated, drunk with the wildness of it. Yet even in the wonder, we didn't completely abandon common sense, so we swam beneath the raised dock, deciding to wait it out *in* the water, yet *under* the dock. That is, Joel, Ben, and I did. Josiah apparently heard mom's voice in his head at full volume with all its inflection and decided to towel off. He waited it out like a civilized person—under a roof and dry.

Discovering His Presence

Oh my God, You are such a holy love, enough,
But still I must have more, lying here on Your sanctuary floor.

I lay in bed with Ethan, his head resting on my arm. We listened to the storm blowing just outside his window. Ethan was nine.

Ethan loves football. He thinks about it at least half of the time. For years our bedtime routine has involved a homemade game. I lay on the bed and he sits next to me. One of us will throw a football up to the ceiling and then we play receiver/defender and wrestle over the ball while Ethan gives the commentary—"Interception!" or "The ball is loose," or "Clark has stripped the ball away," which we both giggle at because we're both named Clark, or "Touchdown," and "The crowd goes wild!"

Normally bedtime becomes a frenzied father-son wrestling match. But on that night we just lay motionless, mesmerized by the wind-whipped rain that was being hurtled against the house. Earlier we had stood on the front porch spellbound by the power of the storm. To us it seemed a small miracle that the trees in our front yard weren't ripped out of the ground and flung like matchsticks at the neighboring houses.

I finally broke the silence. "Ethan, what's your heavenly Father saying to you right now?"

"He loves me?" he said, looking at me for conformation.

I confirmed it with a hug. "He does! Do you believe Him?"

My beautiful boy grinned, "Yes." And he did. I could see it all over his face.

"Do you know that He is pleased with you? Do you know that He finds you amazing, and His greatest desire is that you believe and know His always-good love?"

Ethan listened quietly; we were having a God-moment. "Do you know that He is in this room, His very presence?"

We lay a while longer, peaceful in the midst of a storm.

Finally Ethan asked the question I'd set up. "Dad, how do you know when God is speaking to you; how do you know His presence?"

"Bud, our heavenly Father's presence is always with us and He is always speaking to us. And He is always saying one thing: 'I love you.'"

I waited a moment, as the storm continued its powerful display, to let it settle and then added, "Our heavenly Father is always asking one question too. Do you know what it is?"

He shook his head.

"He's asking, do you believe me?"

"Son, if you want to become more aware of His presence, it starts with believing that He loves you."

I have discovered that to know and become aware of my heavenly Father in greater measure, I must become convinced in my theology that God is love and He is always good. When I lean into this faith, when I live expecting His goodness regardless of my circumstances, then my heart is open for an encounter, a revelation, a new experience with the power of His love. I have learned that the extent to which I'm convinced He is love is the extent that I can recognize when Love is in the room. And He *is* always in the room!

I am growing daily in my awareness of my Father's love. It's my life's one true ambition. I would like to suggest it's yours as well. This life is about recognizing, knowing, and becoming love—in that order. And it is a journey.

And this journey into His love starts with simply saying yes. It's the same yes you said that first glorious day you knew your salvation.

It's the yes that says my Father loves me, His love is good, and His love is more than enough. While many would like to tell you the journey has changed or grown more complicated, while many have allowed disappointment to devastate and reduce love to a concept, a feeling, or a physiological need, they are simply wrong.

We exist to know the answer to the question; we live to become sure in His love.

Throughout this book, there may be moments where you feel a desire to encounter more of the Father's always-good love. That desire is what His presence feels like. In that moment, you are sensing His pursuit of you. When this happens, I would be honored if you would stop reading and simply invite the Father to reveal more of His love to you.

Because I believe He will. And it may be as beautifully obvious as a Scripture verse or as wonderfully mysterious as a chill running down your spine, but you will know. He knows how best to communicate to you. And it will be good. Why? Because God is love, His love is always good, and you were created to become sure in His love.

Recognizing and saying yes to His love is the most profound and impactful thing we will ever do. Of this I am convinced. Knowing His love is the key to living fully free, a life of faith, a life where every dream is available and every impossibility is made possible.

A Million Miles Away

Fill Your lungs and breathe on me,
I want to feel You like You're in the room.

"Jason, how do you do that?" my friend asked. Before I could respond, he continued. "You talk about God like He's your best friend, like He's in this room sitting at our table, like He is talking to you all the time." He paused for a moment and I could see he was distressed. "I have been saved since I was five," he continued, "and I don't feel like I really know what you are talking about. Most days, God seems like He is a million miles away."

This fella and I go back several years. We have had some incredible discussions about God's love. He is a wild believer. He is a church leader. And he is a man of God. He wasn't challenging me; he was exposing a great hunger in his heart, a hunger for a deeper relationship with Father God, for authentic encounters with Love.

Gently, I asked a question, "Bro, are you convinced, head to toes, that He is absolutely, unwaveringly, always in love with you?"

Through sudden tears, he responded, "I have been taught about God's love. I know the Scriptures, so I am sure here." He pointed to his head. "But the way you talk about His love, I feel like I am missing something. Honestly, I'm not always sure here," pointing to his heart.

I don't think my friend is alone. There is an epidemic ravaging the hearts of many believers. We are head rich and heart hungry. I have met too many Christians who've rarely felt intimate with the Father and are daily battling overwhelming doubts about His uncompromising, personal, one-of-a-kind love. I have met too many believers who are desperately hungry for an encounter that includes more than their intellect.

I think this journey we are all on is about becoming sure in our heavenly Father's love. I am convinced that we are created to taste and to touch, to see and to hear, to discover and to know His goodness—His presence. And not just occasionally.

The Lake, Part Three

We stood chest deep in water beneath the dock. The storm didn't disappoint. The rain was falling so heavy that we couldn't even see ten yards. I was a boy again, making jokes, laughing; and though I didn't sing, I came close. We told stories about people getting struck by lightning—each one of us trying to better the previous tale.

"You know how they say that lightning never strikes in the same place twice?" Ben was speaking loudly, almost yelling over the sound of the mighty storm. "There is a guy I read about who was struck seven times and lived!"

"That's awesome!" I laughed.

Joel yelled, "I just read a statistic that stated nine out of ten people struck by lightning actually survive."

I opened my mouth, ready with a joke, you know, something like, "Well, there's only three of us in the water; those seem like pretty good odds!" But my brothers would have to miss my clever banter as it was in that exact moment that I became disoriented. It was in that moment that a spear seemed to plunge straight through my heart.

I choked out a scream as a jolt of pain shot through my entire body.

At the exact same moment, both Ben and Joel also appeared to have been speared. Pain and confusion painted their faces. Ben started laughing but it had become panicked in tone. Joel, slightly hunched over, yelled, "Get out of the water!" He started for the steps leading up to the covered dock. He was laughing now as well, but it also hinted at hysteria. I watched dumb as he plowed through the water trying to understand what had just happened. Then I heard the crack of lightning and the boom of thunder. I followed Joel and Ben up the steps, my laughter joining theirs. Mom's voice couldn't have been louder if she'd been standing next to us screaming.

"Joel, is my head smoking?" I asked.

Later, Josiah, who had watched the whole thing from the dry safety of the covered dock, said that the lightning had struck the lake only thirty feet from us.

The Power of Love

When the Spirit moves, comes like a hurricane.
Falls like fire, soaks like rain...

I know many who can hypothesize about Love. I know many who can debate the theology, they can tell me the Greek definitions and Hebrew pronunciations, and there is nothing wrong with that. There is true beauty in loving God with our all of our minds. But infinitely more important is loving God with our all of our heart. Love's not rote discipline; it's a response birthed from an encounter, from a revelation of our heavenly Father.

Jesus said, *"Love the Lord your God with all your heart and with all your soul and with all your strength and with all your mind"* (Luke 10:27). There's a reason it's in that order. We are to be heart-first lovers.

It's foolish to stand in a lightning storm. I understand that. But the metaphor works. God's love is beautiful, but its beauty is truly discovered in its power. While His love can be felt in the gentle breeze, His love *is* all the power of the thunderstorm. And I have been ruined. I have stood in love's downpour and I have been speared through with love's great passion for me. I have tasted love; I've drowned in it—baptized and redeemed. I am becoming sure, head to toes, that He loves me absolutely and the life I dream of is found in a greater encounter with my Father in heaven, a greater revelation.

His love is the most beautiful and sustaining reality in life. And I will always speak about Him like He's in the room because He is in the room. He is here. In this very moment, His love is more than a nice idea or concept. His love has the power to transform. His love is in the gentle whisper and, when embraced, it will surround us, it will spear us through, it will transform us, and it will change absolutely everything.

When I live in love's downpour, when I can see my Father, I am transformed to live in the power of His love. I have written this book as an invitation for you to join me out in the power of the storm. Let's believe that God is love and His love is always good. Let's grow confident and sure in our Father's love for us. Let's trust and risk and grow in our faith.

Let's live in the pursuit of greater intimacy with our heavenly Father. Let's become sons and daughters with all of heaven at our beck and call. Let's discover a love that is always beautiful, always powerful, always dangerous, wholly unexplainable, and absolutely glorious!

Remember: God is always saying, "I love you."

And He's always asking, "Do you believe Me?"

BIGGER THAN THE FUTURE

I See an Ociton

I heard Your voice and it sounded like the wind.
—Band of a Thousand[1]

Several years ago Eva and I went to the "city town." Eva was two at the time. Eva is my favorite. On the drive in I began to sing an old song I woke up humming that morning. It was a song I hadn't heard in years. The lyrics captivated me.

I love You, Lord
And I lift my voice
To worship You
Oh, my soul rejoice!
Take joy my King
In what You hear
Let it be a sweet, sweet sound in Your ear.[2]

I couldn't stop singing the last line: "Let it be a sweet, sweet sound…"

That morning I woke up feeling heavy and very alone. As soon as my eyes opened I was thinking about all that had to be done, the needs of my family, and the needs of the business. But mostly, I thought about the language barrier between God and myself. "God, I need You. I'm desperate for You," I said. And while I knew He could hear me—Him being God and all—it felt like I was speaking into a vast space, my plea an infinite echo.

Let me give a little backstory. A year earlier, while I was out for a run, I felt God speak to my heart. This had become an almost daily occurrence. I was in a beautiful season, my business was thriving, my relationships were beautiful, my family blessed, and God felt closer than my skin. His presence was very real.

Like all my God-encounters, He expressed His love and pleasure over Karen, the kids, and me. However, as I was nearing home, the conversation took an extremely uncomfortable turn. As I asked God what was on His heart for the coming days, I felt Him say, "Jason, I am going into hiding, and I am removing your friends."

I know what you are thinking: "That doesn't sound like something God would say." I thought the same thing too. I actually challenged the thought. But as I walked into the house, I couldn't shake it.

I want to make this clear: I believe to my core that God will never leave or forsake me. But since that run I also know that sometimes God hides.

Within six months of that conversation, our closest friends had all announced and then moved to other states—all for different but no less God-led reasons. Our sweet community was no more. Within days of that conversation, God went into stealth mode. I couldn't have described it at the time as anything other than "God's gone." I knew it wasn't true but it sure felt that way.

Hindsight allows for a better description. It was like He went into another room and started whispering a foreign language through the wall. His voice was muted, His presence obscured.

I had my Bible and I had the foundations and principles of thirty-some years, but His presence, the sense of closeness with Him that I had come to love, felt absent, just a memory. My faith was being challenged in a new way.

A year later I had run through the ten steps of grieving and developed a couple of new ones. I read my Bible and had faith that He was with me. I believed it like I believe coffee is best when served with a slice of strawberry rhubarb pie or like I believe the Music City Miracle was a forward pass or like I believe Radiohead's best album was *OK Computer*. God is always with us—always. But I was desperate for a sense of His presence, His pleasure, His love. I was well past discouraged.

One day I drove to "city town" on a business errand with my two-year-old. And by faith I was singing to my heavenly Father, "Take joy my King, in what You hear."

Eva corrected, "No, Daddy." She started singing, "B-I-N-E-O! B-I-N-E-O! And Binno was his name-o." I changed my song and joined in hers. "B-I-N-E-O," we sang with abandon. Eva couldn't pronounce the *g*, but I was all right replacing the *g* with an *e*.

We arrived at "city town," and while Eva pointed out all the red "ocitons," which are stop signs, I began to pray—a list of needs a desperate mile long.

Eva broke into my thoughts, "Daddy, I aff a secret. Let's go a mdonals." I smiled. She was so beautiful; it made me ache with goodness. She wanted to go to McDonald's with her Daddy and have it be our secret. What made it even sweeter is that she can't keep a secret.

"Okay, let's go eat," I said to Eva after finishing my errands. We didn't go to McDonald's, but we did stop at Phat Burrito, which is one of the best eats in "city town." I told Eva the name of the restaurant while we waited in line. I told her again while we got a Coke. I shared my quesadilla. As Eva ate she asked, "Daddy, what's this?" And then "Fat bummito!"

I smiled. "That's right, hun, it's a fat bummito."

While we ate, my mind wandered again. When God "disappeared," I spent months offended, then months repenting, then months giving Him everything. None of that changed His mind. He continued to be hidden, He continued to speak muffled through a wall in a foreign language. I was so hungry for God's clear voice, for His overwhelming good presence. I needed Him!

As Eva and I headed home, I prayed out loud: "God, I need to hear Your voice. Please speak to my heart like You have done so many times before. I am desperate for You!" Then Eva interrupted, "Daddy, I see a ociton," and suddenly I became emotional.

When you love someone, you learn to speak their language. I am Eva's dad and I know her from head to toes. I love her fiercely and intimately. And I am fluent in her language. I often speak it to her. But she is also learning a language—mine.

The thought crossed my mind: "If God is speaking and I can't understand Him, then it's time to learn a new language." By faith, I began to sing again.

Take joy my King
In what You hear.
Let it be a sweet, sweet sound in Your ear.

It would be another year before I began to understand our new love language. Some of that revelation would happen while out on another run, where God would ask me if He was a good Father. And this new language, it would be the invitation to know His always-good love, it would be an invitation to become sure.

A New Language

I hide food. You might find a bag of Sweet and Spicy Jalapeno Cape Cod chips under the seat of my car. You might discover a Coffee Crisp chocolate bar, courtesy of my mom's latest visit to Canada, in the back of my nightstand drawer. You might even discover a can of Coke in the cupboard above the fridge.

And yes, sometimes I act surprised that I bought the hot salsa even when I knew it was the hot salsa. Why? Because I am the only person in the house that likes the salsa hot and because I have a son who is always "starving."

Many years ago, when Ethan was four, he woke Karen and me up in the morning to tell us, "Stay in bed, I won't eat all the sticky buns." He lied.

Hypothetically: If I were to come home with four donuts, any or all of my three amazing and generous children might act as if there were a worldwide donut crisis. Including myself, there are five people who live in my house, but, "Seriously, Dad, four donuts?"

Earth revolves around need; earth's math is solid, its measurements true. If you have five people and everyone wants their own donut, you either need five donuts or someone has to go without…and that's why I hide things.

But there is a greater truth, a greater revelation that trumps the math of need.

> *Taking the five loaves and the two fish and looking up to heaven, He gave thanks and broke them. Then He gave them to the disciples to set before the people. They all ate and were satisfied, and the disciples picked up twelve basketfuls of broken pieces that were left over* (Luke 9:16-17).

I bet Jesus didn't hide stuff. He didn't need to. He lived from heaven to earth where need was a foreign concept. He lived in the measureless need-trumping love of His Father.

I don't know about you, but I have lived a great portion of my life from earth to heaven. My understanding of my need has been, for the most part, greater than my revelation of His love. I have done most of my thinking, talking, praying, and worshiping in the limitations of need, both with God and the world around me.

I have related to my Father in heaven and others through the lens of limited resources. I have confined heaven to the measurements of earth and I have discovered that if the reality of need, the limited resources of earth, is my compass, insecurity is a daily companion.

Insecurity can lead to strange bedfellows, so to speak. Insecurity is often the invitation to a wrestling match with feelings of hopelessness, envy, greed, lust, and all the other desperations of need. When need is bigger than love, dysfunction will worm its way into every relationship.

When we live from the limited resources of earth, we will intrinsically believe that for one person to have, another must go without; for one to be blessed, another must be cursed; for one to experience joy, another must know sorrow; for one to have peace, another must be oppressed; for one to be rich, another must be poor, and so on.

It's the exact opposite of what Jesus revealed. In the measureless revelation of heaven, the last are also first, the weak are also strong, and those that give, receive.

There were no limited resources in Jesus's reality; there were no limits to His love, generosity, mercy, grace, healing, hope, and life. There were no needs Love couldn't trump, no measurements that couldn't be surpassed.

Jesus taught us a new language. Jesus was a new language. He walked the earth as the Father's love perfectly revealed. He was surrounded by the question of need and lived as the answer—Love. He taught us a new language—the measureless perfection of our Father's need trumping always-good love.

Bigger than the Future

I'm consumed 'neath heaven's crush.

It was bedtime and I was snuggling Eva. I told her a story about a bunny princess named Gertrude who only wore plaid, and a squirrel prince named Hank who only wore pajamas. I paused for the expected interruption and then listened, smiling to tears, as Eva made her revisions. Gertrude became Lizzy with a beautiful pink dress. Hank became Lizzy's best friend Molly. She too had a beautiful dress, hers was purple—and they also had ponies. And as Eva imagined out loud, I thanked my Father for the wonder of this girl. In that moment, I knew love like I never had before.

We transitioned from story time into our closing goodnight communion.

"Eva, you're my favorite. I love you best," I said. It's a family phrase, a motto. I say this to all my kids. And it's true, every time.

"I love you best too, Daddy," she responded and the game had begun.

"I love you to the tops of the trees." I smiled.

"I love you to the tops of the trees and the moon, times a hundred." She knows how to play.

"I love you to the moon and stars and universe and back, times a hundred and five," I grinned back at her.

She giggled, "I love you to the moon, the stars, the universe, and back, times a hundred and ten!"

We continued for a few more minutes, each taking turns surpassing the last statement, a million, billion, gazillion, eternity, to infinity and beyond.

Many of you know the pure joy of this game. You have played it with your loved one. It never loses its wonder.

I don't know if you have ever thought of it this way, but this is a game of measurements. The beautiful thing is, love is immeasurable. Every time Eva and I play this game, we do our best to measure love and discover to our immense joy that it can't be done.

Eva always ends our competition with an amazing statement. The first time she said it, I was stunned. Now it's the phrase that suspends the conversation until we wake the next morning: "I love you bigger than the future."

> *And I pray that you, being rooted and established in love, may*
> *have power, together with all the saints, to grasp how wide*
> *and long and high and deep is the love of Christ, and to know*
> *this love that surpasses knowledge—that you may be filled to*
> *the measure of all the fullness of God* (Ephesians 3:17-19).

I can't imagine how Paul felt trying to describe a love that is bigger than the future—a love that surpasses knowledge. But I bet it felt a little like the game Eva and I play at bedtime.

Paul starts by using the language of earth. It's as if he is saying Christ's love is *wider* than forever, *longer* than eternity, *higher* than a million, billion, gazillion, and *deeper* than infinity times a hundred.

Paul invites us into an encounter with God's bigger-than-the-future love so that we may *"be filled to the measure of all the fullness of God."* Measurements are the stuff of earth. To measure we use words like wide, long, high, and deep, words like filled and fullness.

But once Paul has done his absolute best to measure the love of God, he shifts into the language of heaven. In the next breath Paul expands our revelation.

> *Now to Him who is able to do immeasurably more than all*
> *we ask or imagine, according to His power that is at work*
> *within us...* (Ephesians 3:20).

Paul essentially says, "I want you to be filled to the full measure of the immeasurable." And just in case we might be tempted to try and apply measurements to the immeasurable, Paul added "beyond" and "all," as if to say, "Stop it, you can't measure Love. He surpasses knowledge!"

Measurements are something that make perfect sense on earth but are a foreign concept in heaven. Heaven operates in the economy of love and love is bigger than the future. I believe this Scripture is an invitation to move from the measurable reality of earth to the immeasurable revelation of heaven. And I would like to suggest that's why Jesus came. Jesus didn't live simply to reveal a destination, He showed us the foundation—our Father's perfect love.

Jesus never lived for the immeasurable; He lived from it. Jesus demonstrated what a bigger-than-the-future love could look like. And He invited us to know and live it like He did. Immeasurable was never just meant to be a destination; it's always been His heart that it would be our foundation.

Need is measurable; it's the stuff of earth. Love is immeasurable; it's the economy of heaven. Love trumps need. Our life on earth is the only time we will ever be given the opportunity to live from heaven.

Thy Kingdom come…bigger than the future.

Intimacy

There's no place I'd rather be,
Than singing love to You as You're singing over me.

I leaned in close to my beautiful Karen. Her back was resting against the railing that separated us from the waterfall. This was the girl I would spend the rest of my life with, and I knew it. Earlier, we had walked through the small New York town of Rush. We held hands and laughed. We dreamed and ate chocolate. Now we were hidden from the whole world beneath the fir trees, our very own secret hideaway. And we kissed. It was sweet, magical, beautiful, tender, affectionate, promising—all the things a good kiss should be. And in that moment, I knew Jesus and encountered my Father's love like I never had before. Karen is my favorite, I love her best.

One of the reasons I married Karen was because I needed her, every part of her. As Jerry McGuire said so well, "She completes me."

It's the truth. It's a healthy absolute. I am truly lost without her. I need her mind, her compassion, her patience, her wisdom, her revelation, her smile, her…well, just you never mind.

And it isn't wrong to need her. But if our relationship were built solely on needs met, it would eventually collapse into a legal partnership, a business relationship, a sterile agreement to cohabitation. If needs met is what defines our interactions, at some point our love will grow apathetic and cold, at some point we will fall out of love.

If I only interacted with Karen when I needed her, it would break her heart.

If we only love God for what He can do for us, if our love revolves around needs met, our love will grow stale, lukewarm. And if we aren't in a growing discovery of love, received and given, we will end up relating to Him through the dysfunction of need.

Marriage is meant to be an intimate covenant of love. When love is at the center of a relationship, it's not about what I can get out of it, it's about what I can give. And the generous truth in this relationship is not only are needs met, but needs are exceeded in the measureless abundance of love.

If Karen and I only loved each other because of needs met, we would miss out on intimacy. Intimacy is the greatest expression of love between two people. I am not just writing about the physical either. Intimacy is available in every aspect of a relationship where love is the foundation.

Intimacy is way bigger then needs met. It is about revelation. Karen and I have been married nearly twenty years and she is more fascinating to me today than yesterday. The more I know her, the more I want to know her. The wonder of intimacy is the discovery of a measureless love.

Revelation, in the context of a love relationship, will always lead to a greater intimacy—bigger than the future.

Father Friend

I coached Ethan's football team and stood on the field the day he intercepted the ball in our end zone by wrestling it from his opponent's hands. I leapt and screamed like a mad man as he turned and ran the entire field to score a touchdown. When I finally caught up to the jumping, cheering boy in the end zone, I put my forehead to his and looked into his eyes, and I knew love like I never had before.

I love Ethan. He is my son and he is my best friend. The other day, while we were resting in bed after a good wrestling match, I reminded him he was my favorite, I loved him best. And then I told him something my dad had said to me, something that marked me in the measureless love between father and son.

I told Ethan, "You're my best friend."

I think I was fifteen the first time my dad introduced me as his son and *friend*. I remember how I felt, the expansion of my heart; it was true. My dad is my hero; he is everything I want to become. He is a godly man and he is my best friend. I am blessed.

My dad never stopped being my dad the day he introduced me as his friend, he simply expanded my revelation of the love between father and son. I continued to follow my dad's instruction and come to him with my needs. As we have both matured in our relationship, I have continued to look to him for wisdom and he will always hold a place of authority in my life. He is my dad.

The day he introduced me as a friend didn't change the fact that my dad loves meeting my needs. I am nearly forty and he and mom still leave checks when they visit. Mom still finds joy in buying me a coat or a pair of jeans. She is my mom. But my relationship with my parents is greater than the sum of my needs met. We are best friends.

Love the Lord...

I understand how my dad and mom feel; I have three kids of my own.

I stood mesmerized with Maddy, my firstborn beauty. Her head in my upturned palm, her eyes penetrating my soul, her long body stretched down the length of my forearm, her little legs hanging, straddled at my elbow. When her tiny fingers wrapped around mine, I encountered love like I never had before.

I would love her with a passion and fullness that could only be surpassed by our heavenly Father. Madeleine is my favorite , I love her best.

When Madeleine was born, need was the language of her love. She needed Karen and me for everything, and we revealed our love by meeting all her needs. But Maddy turned one, and two, and so on. And as she matures into an amazing young teenage woman, our love language has matured as well. While we still reveal our love through the meeting of her needs, it is no longer the only way we interact with each other.

We have become best friends, with shared stories and interests and dreams and passions. She will never stop being our girl, *my* girl. We will always be available to help her meet needs; it will always be a foundational language of our love. But my greatest desire isn't that my daughter loves me because I meet her needs, but that she loves me because I love her.

And she does. And for that I am blessed. It's bigger than the future.

I'm convinced our Father's greatest desire isn't that we need Him, it's that we love Him. Jesus didn't tell us to need *"the Lord your God with all your heart and with all your soul and with all your strength and with all your mind"* (Luke 10:27). He said we were to love.

Our Father perfectly values our need; it's a healthy part of our relationship with Him. But as we grow in relationship, need becomes less the language by which He desires to relate with us. As we grow in our Father's love, we begin to understand He doesn't just want a relationship defined by needs met, He wants to be our best friend. And that may mean expanding our vocabulary.

An Expanding Vocabulary

I've been Your echo, I've been Your shadow,
But my heart is to know You so I can be Your voice.

"Blessed are those who hunger and thirst for righteousness,
for they will be filled" (Matthew 5:6).

I love this Scripture because it comes with a promise. If I will hunger, He will fill me.

"For the kingdom of God is…righteousness, peace and joy in
the Holy Spirit" (Romans 14:17).

I love this Scripture because it describes the Kingdom of heaven. And I love that those who hunger and thirst for *righteousness*—the Kingdom of God—shall be filled.

I am hungry for God. I can't measure it, as it's a veracious hunger that is bigger than the future. And I like that word—hunger—much more than desperate. It suggests health. My hunger is not an agreement with desperate need, it's a passion to be filled with the measureless love of my Father. My hunger is actually a healthy awareness that all my needs are answered in a greater revelation of His love. And therefore I must know more!

Need will always be with me but it doesn't have to define me. I am leaning into a greater revelation, a truer language—the love of my Father. And I am convinced that the Christian life is not meant to revolve around need, but is instead a headlong daring discovery of His love.

I am no longer going to live in a relationship that is defined by insecurity. I am learning a new language, one that surpasses knowledge, one that is bigger than the future, a language of heaven to earth.

I love You, Father, not just for how amazing You are at meeting my needs, but because You love me so well. Let my life be a love song to You. Increase my vocabulary, teach me this new language, and "take joy my King, in what You hear. Let it be a sweet, sweet sound in Your ear."

Love Trumps

If I could give one hope, new breath to an old song,
It's a yes that births a more that never ends.

Jesus didn't come to set us straight on how much we needed Him. That was abundantly clear from the moment Adam and Eve ate the forbidden fruit. He came to give us access to love—receiving and giving, beholding and becoming.

While the seen world operates around the measurements of need, the unseen world, the one we are invited to live in by faith, is about measureless love. The Kingdom of heaven operates in the context of love. Our Father does not need us nor is it His greatest desire that we need Him. He is not looking for slaves but for sons and daughters, brothers and sisters, friends.

Need is not a reality in the Kingdom of heaven. We are called to live heaven here, now. The Christian life is about knowing and becoming love, and then meeting the needs of those around us with the love we have received from God. It's a journey into a mature love that has the power of all of heaven at its back.

Need is self-focused. If it's our foundation, then in every interaction we will protect our right to need. If need is the foundation of our relationship with God, we relegate ourselves to a poverty existence. For those consumed by need, God's love is a limited resource, heaven is a remote future, and life, hope, and peace are distant realities that must be striven for.

In the measureless generosity of our Father's love, needs are not just met, they are miraculously redeemed. The reality of heaven transforms the reality on earth. Fear, insecurity, shame, condemnation, every life-taxing fruit of need bends the knee and love trumps. These moments become rally points for revival, testimonies of His nature.

When You Love Someone

Put Your hand upon my head,
I want to feel You like You're in the room.

We were facing bankruptcy. Our business was upside down, I was waking to phone calls, angry vendors, angry bill collectors, and angry customers. In the midst of that, God remained hidden in the next room mumbling through the wall.

If I was being honest, I was angry with God and at myself for being angry with Him. I would go for a run at night and cry out, "Where are You, God? Why would You hide from me? I need You, I am desperate for You! Where are You?"

It was just over two years that God hid from me. Two years where every prayer felt like a one-sided conversation. I knew He loved me, I knew it wasn't anything I had done. I knew His love was too great to ever leave me or forsake me. I knew He was with me. But I felt desperately alone. I wrestled between anxiety and a holy frustration.

In that season my trust was given the opportunity to expand, my hunger was made pure, and grace matured.

Over those two years, and in the years that have followed, I have learned a new language. It's been a language between friends, a shared dreaming.

When you love someone, you learn their language. This language has been an invitation to know the immeasurable love of an always-good Father. It has been an invitation to become sure. It has been an invitation to know love like I never have before...

Bigger than the future.

Notes

1. For more information about this band, please visit http://www.bandofathousand.com.
2. "I Love You, Lord," written by Laurie Klein, 1978, 1980 House of Mercy Music (Maranatha! Music). All rights reserved. International copyright secured. Used by permission.

LOOK UP AND LET GO

An Identity Book?

When I was discussing this book with a friend who works in the publishing world, I told her it was a book about identity. She responded as graciously and kindly as possible and said, "Jason, there are thousands of books on identity. What makes you think we need another?"

I thought for a second and then I said, "This isn't a book on identity, it's a book on the nature of our heavenly Father. Identity is just the by-product."

NYC

Outside of Love and desperate in need.

Grand Central Terminal. Spring of 1993, late afternoon.

"I'm here!" I thought to myself.

"Don't look up and don't let go of your bags," echoed in my head.

It was a new beginning, a beautiful day! After an eighteen-hour bus ride, I arrived to meet my new employer in the greatest city in world history. At least, that's what New Yorkers always tell me. I'd been hired to be a roadie for Phil Driscoll, one of the world's greatest trumpet players. At least that's what Doc Severinson said (famed trumpeter for the Johnny Carson show).

"The terminal feels dirty," I thought as I got off the bus. I was comparing it to all the movies I'd watched over the years, but mostly to *Superman*. "Well not really dirty, just used," I revised as I nervously eyed my fellow travelers while wondering what I should do next.

"Don't look up and don't let go of your bags," shot through my head again.

I had twenty-nine dollars and thirty-one cents in my pocket. I'd started out with thirty dollars, but the Reese's Peanut Butter Cup at one of the stops in western New York State had called out to me. It had been a nice touch to the potato chips, apple, and peanut butter and honey sandwich Mom had packed for me.

My folks didn't have any money at the time of my New York trip, and this was before credit cards were a way of life. So I had just enough cash to buy the twenty-five dollar ticket back to Rochester in case my employer ended up being a no-show.

Everyone was heading out of the station. I stood next to the bus, paralyzed by fear. My Walkman was still attached to my hip, U2's "Joshua Tree" blaring: "I still haven't found what I'm looking for..."

I had been hired as a roadie. Two months earlier I didn't even know what a roadie was.

I had left home confident that I was mature enough to be on my own. Then again, two months earlier I borrowed money from my dad to buy a garage sale Atari system.

I had looked at a map before leaving, sure that I could navigate New York City. Then again, two months earlier I'd lost my car in a mall parking lot. What if I went in the wrong direction?

I realized I had to make a decision. I put away the Walkman, clutched my bags, kept my head down, and joined the flow one timid step at a time. I felt nothing like Superman but a lot like Clark Kent.

Eventually I found myself standing on Park Ave.—the same Park Ave. that had eluded me in many family Monopoly games, except this Park Ave. had thousands of frustrated people pushing past each other while hundreds of yellow cabs blasted horns and whizzed by.

I was eighteen years old and had never been alone in a city of this size. I was internalizing terror while feigning casual boredom. I was insecure and unsure. I was in crisis.

Then I heard it again: "Don't look up and don't let go of your bags."

If You've Seen Me

You're gonna run with the sons of thunder,
Taste and see the love of Father.

There are no verses in the Bible where Jesus stood paralyzed in fear next to a Greyhound bus while questioning everything about Himself. I'm not saying you couldn't surprise Jesus; I believe you could. The woman with the issue of blood surprised Him (see Luke 8:43), but He wasn't surprised by the fact that His Father healed her. His Father's always-good love never surprised Him. He was surprised, though, by the woman's bold faith.

And I'm not saying Jesus never faced paralyzing fear—He did. He fully experienced fear while sweating blood in the garden before going to the cross. But He was never paralyzed by the fear. Jesus was sure in His Father's love and His identity as His Son.

And that's my point: Jesus could be surprised but was anxious for nothing. He could experience fear but never once succumbed to it. Anger, strife, persecution, accusation, sickness, hunger, lack of faith, death, sin, sin, and more sin—nothing seemed to shake His security. He was absolutely certain of His Father's good love and His identity as His Son.

I think Jesus was sure for one reason: He was *in* the Father and the Father was *in* Him (see John 14:11). Jesus said, *"Anyone who has seen Me has seen the Father"* (John 14:9). He also said, *"I tell you the truth, the Son can do nothing by Himself; He can do only what He sees His Father doing, because whatever the Father does the Son also does"* (John 5:19). Then Jesus walked the planet as the Father's love perfectly revealed. And it's what you would expect considering *"God is love"* (1 John 4:8).

I believe there are two certainties to which we have access because of Jesus's life, death, and resurrection. Everyone pretty much knows the first. It's been the primary focus within the church for two thousand years; it's the absolutely stunning certainty of salvation.

I would like to suggest that the second certainty is just as brilliant. Jesus showed us what a life could look like when a son or daughter knows their heavenly Dad. He lived, died, and rose to reveal our Father, and what a life could look like when we are sure in our identity as His kids.

He modeled for us what we have access to as sons and daughters of an always-good and loving Father. He came to reveal not just love, but also what it looks like to become love. He lived, died, and rose again so we too could be sure.

But the crazy thing is that though I gave my heart to Jesus when I was five, I lived much of the following thirty years in the ache of insecurity, always on the cusp of an identity crisis.

Bob Mumford

I grew up in one of the most privileged homes in the world. Both my dad and mom love God with all their hearts, souls, minds, and strength. They love each other and their kids the same way. My dad and mom are true saints. They are faithful believers. Therefore, I grew up with an overwhelming advantage—I knew love and was raised in love from my very first breath.

I know what a good dad and mom looks like, acts like, hugs like, encourages like, laughs like...the list is longer than this book could contain. And yet even with such an amazing experience and understanding of what a good dad and mom are, I spent much of my first thirty years insecure, unsure, and in search of my Father.

"Remind me, who is Bob Mumford?" my roommate Doug asked me one day.

"Bob Mumford is a man of God," I said incredulous. "And he's coming here!" I was excited. If you have ever had the opportunity to meet one of your real-life heroes, then you know what I was feeling.

It was my second year of Bible college and Bob Mumford had been invited to speak. He came for the aptly titled "Week of Prayer," which was an entire week dedicated to, well, you guessed it…prayer. Instead of class, we went to a service in the morning, two after lunch, and one in the evening. Over the course of the week, we prayed for pretty much everything a person can pray for. During the week the entire school grew in love with God and in vision for both our nation and our world.

The "Week of Prayer" was good, which is important when every service is mandatory. But it was also long. I spent most of my days in deep meditation. I was pretty good at finding a nice section of floor. I would lie down on my stomach, rest my forehead on my Bible, and mostly pray.

"If I can just carry his bags when he arrives at the airport, I think it would make me holier," I said to Doug. I wasn't positive that's how holiness worked, but it couldn't hurt.

"Those must be some powerful bags," Doug said sarcastically.

"You don't get it," I responded, shaking my head. "This guy is just a step or three below the Trinity."

Doug finally showed the proper respect. "I guess I'd carry his bags too, then."

"Yeah, he probably wouldn't let you."

I had many heroes growing up. They were the typical '80s fare— Superman, Indiana Jones, MacGyver. But because of my amazing

God-loving parents, I also had a few Christian heroes. They were my dad's heroes first, but my dad had an incredible influence on his kids.

There was Keith Green, the radical singer/songwriter revolutionary. There was Phil Driscoll, the growling anointed trumpet virtuoso. And then there was Bob Mumford.

Bob Mumford was a man of God. I knew this because my dad told me so. My dad was a man of God himself, this I knew firsthand; so if anyone would know what a man of God looked like, it would be my dad.

Bob was a gifted speaker, a storyteller, and author with incredible revelation directly from heaven. But as a kid, more importantly, Bob was funny.

My dad said that Bob loved to make you laugh so he could punch you in the teeth without splitting your lip. I wasn't sure why Bob wanted to punch me in the teeth, but I loved to laugh, especially with my dad, and Bob did the trick.

When the day finally arrived, I was as giddy as a schoolboy. Giddiness isn't just for the girls, you know. I remember when Bob walked onto the stage before the service started. He was laughing with one of our teachers. My heart clutched and I prayed sincerely, "God, if I could just carry that man's bags." He wasn't carrying any bags at the moment, but I was pretty sure God understood what I meant.

When Bob spoke, it was incredible. Bob was funny. We all laughed heartily, everyone, but most of all me. Bob was also filled with revelation. The message was profound and beautiful; I got punched in the teeth. "Dad is right!" I thought, "Bob is a man of God!"

After the service I really wanted to talk to him. I desperately wanted this man of God to lay his hands on my head and bless me with all the authority of heaven. I couldn't explain it at the time, but I was practically paralyzed with the need to be seen, to be valued, to be considered righteous and good. Looking back, I realize that I ached to discover and be discovered by my Father. I was in crisis, and at that moment I somehow thought Bob was the answer.

I thought about going up to Bob, but there were lots of important people around him. I stood on the fringe of the swarming crowd, scared, unsure, and waiting for the hullabaloo to die down. But eventually I had to go—literally.

I was standing at the urinal, sick of heart, when an older fella walked up to the urinal on my left. I looked over while strictly following urinal protocol, which is eye contact only.

A divine appointment! Bob Mumford was peeing right beside me!

Trying not to hyperventilate, I played it cool and just nodded. I took care of business and headed over to the sink. Proud of myself for not starting a conversation at the urinal, I slowly washed my hands and waited for Bob to join me. He did.

I was nervous. Bob Mumford is a man of God. But I knew it was my only chance. "Brother Mumford?" I said. For those wondering, the school I was attending used "Brother" and "Sister" instead of Mr. or Mrs. as the respectable prefix.

"Yes?" He said with a twinkle in his eye.

"I grew up listening to you preach," I said, happy that he had seen me washing my hands. Maybe he would let me carry his bags.

"Really?" He smiled graciously.

"Any moment now he is going to do it," I thought. What *it* was I couldn't have told you, but *it* was going to settle the ache.

I continued, "I sure appreciate the message you gave us."

"Thank you," he replied and then asked, "Are you a student?"

"Yes." I told Bob a little of my long family history with the school. He actually knew my grandmother. It had to mean something.

He was gracious and friendly, but the interaction was ending, I could feel the anxiety building in me.

"Well, it was nice to meet you, Jason. God bless you!" Bob smiled as he dried his hands with the paper towels. He was a magnificent hand drier.

"Here it is," I thought desperately. And then, well…and then the man of God walked out the bathroom door. Just like that, Bob was gone.

"You too, Brother Mumford!" I hollered as the door closed behind him. I dried my hands and slowly followed, heartsick, overwhelmed by disappointment, and still so unsure. The ache in my heart was beginning to suffocate. I needed, I needed, I needed…

I needed him to pray for me. I needed him to give me some profound word from heaven. I needed him to see me and say, "I recognize the call of God on you. You are a world changer!" I needed to carry his bags. I needed to follow him around as he ministered. I needed his phone number and home address. I needed to be invited to his house for the holidays, where he would tell me he would always keep a spare room ready for me. I needed us to become best friends, maybe get matching T-shirts, and go camping together. I needed to sit with him around a campfire while roasting marshmallows for our waiting graham crackers and chocolate. I needed to eat s'mores with Bob Mumford.

What I needed from Bob was impossible for Bob to give.

You see, I needed him to tell me who I was. I needed the crisis to be settled forever. I didn't want to live paralyzed by fear anymore. I didn't want to feel the ache of insecurity anymore. I longed for someone to make me sure, someone to tell me I was my Father's son, that I was a man of God, a spiritual giant, maybe even like Bob Mumford.

God the Father

I'm gonna go where I know You'll follow.

The world is starving for fathers. I have tasted it in my own life— the insecurity of the orphan. Even though I have a wonderful father and mother, I have chased many "Bob Mumfords," searching for someone to make me sure, someone to answer the question, someone to relieve the ache, someone to settle my haunting crisis of identity.

It's not just my crisis. Everywhere I look I see it. I live in a world that is desperate to know Dad. It surrounds us, engulfs us, this crisis of identity. It is the overwhelming battle we all face. From the tent cities in Haiti to the house down my street, from the orphanage in China to the Sunday morning service around the corner, humanity is living in the ache of fatherlessness. We are in crisis.

It was evident in my friend's seventy-year-old grandfather when she witnessed his gut-wrenching weeping after he heard the news of the death of a father he had never even met. I saw the haunting in the eyes of the four-year-old girl being held by a hurting mother on the front porch while the little girl waved to her weekend daddy as he drove away. I heard it in the voice of a young man of God who leads a small group and is passionate about his faith. It's evidenced in the lives of the rich and the poor. And while it's an obvious issue for those who have not yet said yes to God, oddly it's hardly less prevalent in the church. Humanity aches in the insecurity of fatherlessness.

It was Adam and Eve who did this to us. They cursed us to live in the desperate ache of insecurity. They took their God-given freedom, and yours and mine in the process, and they spit on it. They chose this hell. They chose to trade security for insecurity. They placed the law of need between our Father's love and us. That's what that stupid apple cost us. The knowledge of good and evil positioned humanity to live in the absolute and overwhelming reality of need. The moment they sinned, we all became orphans, stumbling along, scared and unsure, separated from God the Father. There have been days when I've hated them for it.

But "God (the Father) is love" (1 John 4:18). And He is always good. Two thousand years ago, something so remarkable happened that I can't help but grin when I think about it. Jesus, God's only Son, became Love in human form. Then He walked the earth sure in His Father's love and He lived as the Father's love perfectly revealed.

God has more names than there are ice cream flavors. He is the Creator, Shepherd, and Deliverer. He is Holy, Majestic, and Righteous. He is our Peace, Provider, Comforter, and Healer. He is Lord, King, Master, and Savior. The list goes on and on. And while Jesus certainly revealed all of these attributes, they weren't His primary objective. He came for one reason: to reveal the *Father*. But why?

I would like to suggest that our questions, longing, insecurity, and identity are forever answered, settled, satisfied, and secured in our revelation of God as Father.

I have forgiven Adam and Eve; Jesus made that possible. He lived, died, and lived again so that we would no longer have to live as orphans. He settled the crisis of identity forever.

NYC Continued

I found a pay phone. Instead of using more of my precious twenty-nine dollars and thirty-one cents, I called my parents collect. In those days, cell phones weighed twenty pounds and were only used by Michael Douglas.

"I'm here, in New York City!" I said as confidently as possible.

"Is an adult there to pick you up?" my mother asked.

"No, Mom," I answered, outwardly irritated but inwardly thankful by her question. "But I think I will try to hail a cab to the hotel and see if I can find them," I said in my best adult-like voice.

Mom wanted me to buy a return ticket and catch the next Greyhound home. But I was a grown-up now and this was my chance to prove it. I knew what a real adult would do. A real adult would take a cab.

"Don't look up and don't let go of your bags." That was the last piece of advice my dad had said in my ear as he hugged me good-bye the day before.

I clutched my bags and kept my eyes forward, determined not to look up. I wasn't sure what would happen if I looked up, but I knew it must be bad. Determined to hail a cab, determined to get myself to my new employer's hotel—the Marriott Marquis right on Times Square—I walked shyly to the street curb and raised my hand just as I'd seen the adults in the movies do.

The map my dad and I had looked at before I left had shown the hotel to be only four blocks from Grand Central Station. "So this is doable," I thought. The street was filled bumper to bumper with yellow cabs. Still feeling more the bumbling Clark Kent then Superman, I timidly waived my arm. There is nothing timid about NYC. The cabs sped past, unconvinced.

While I stood, attempting to feign boredom, I contemplated my next move. It was then that I noticed something dreadful. I was looking up.

Shocked at how easily I had succumbed, I brought my focus back to street level. I literally jumped back, startled by the older fella whose face was mere inches from mine. He looked to be in his mid-fifties, I couldn't say for sure. His hair was wiry and mostly grey, and he had a distinctly recognizable and unpleasant body odor. But what most stood out was the patchwork of bandages that lined the insides of both arms.

I'd seen that in the movies too. I knew what it meant. This guy was definitely a troublemaker.

"Where are you going?" he asked. He was missing a front tooth, and the one he had was black.

I nodded, "I'm fine, sir, thanks."

He leaned closer. "Need a cab?"

I just wanted him to go away. "I'm fine, please, I mean, thanks."

"Where are you going?" he demanded this time.

"I shouldn't have looked up," I thought once again. And then, because of my good upbringing, I answered the question. "I am staying at the Marriott Marquis on Times Square."

"I know where that is. You don't need a cab. Five bucks and I'll take you there."

Before I could answer, he snatched one of my bags out of my hand and crossed the street.

On a spring day, at the age of eighteen, I timidly followed after a sour-smelling fella through the angry streets of NYC. Cursed at by an old lady for getting in her way, I was jostled, pressed, and bumped as I awkwardly trailed in the wake of my stolen bag.

I was taken to the wrong hotel, told it was the right hotel, cursed at—this time by a cabbie that honestly had every right to be upset as I was forced to either run in front of his car or lose my newly acquired tour guide as well as his newly acquired bag. And finally, I was delivered to the correct hotel.

In the following hours I would meet a mythic trumpet player and his crew, be led through the bowels of Madison Square Garden while the National Democratic Convention for Bill Clinton was winding down, pass by a reporter in an ugly purple coat jacket, recognize that he was the reporter I'd just seen on the hotel TV, as he was still wearing that ugly purple coat jacket, witness the Rev. Jessie Jackson give a speech while standing at the edge of the gay pride parade on Times Square, and then be flown off in a personal King Air (plane) to begin my grand adventure as a roadie to the virtuoso trumpeter, Phil Driscoll.

That's the story of when I left home for the first time, a boldly anxious kid searching for his purpose, his promise, his destiny, his identity, his Father. It was a search I have been on since I took my first breath.

And while my dad's advice might have been great for a young, naïve NYC traveler, I've discovered the best stories, the ones that have my heavenly Father's fingerprints all over them, the ones that reveal my destiny and settle the crisis of identity, are discovered when I do the exact opposite.

For the best stories, you have to look up and you have to let go.

A Good Story

It's deep within my heart, making room for heaven's choir,
Singing Hallelu, Hallelujah, I exhale to breathe You in.
—Band of a Thousand[1]

Jesus lived the best story.

His story is the one where the issue of a Father is forever settled. In His story, He was the hero destined to save the world. In His story, there was an antagonist (you've probably heard of him). There was also a crisis; it's the same crisis that we find in the best of stories. It's the same crisis I have wrestled through, the same crisis that's plagued humankind since Adam and Eve messed things up in the Garden. It's the crisis we face today. From the moment we wake up till the moment we finally rest our heads, it attempts to strangle us. For those who don't know Jesus, this crisis is absolute in its control. But even for those who have said yes to Love, it can often feel overwhelming, smothering us in doubt. It's the crisis of identity.

Jesus faced this crisis like no other human ever has. And He faced it perfectly, always *in* the Father. He never doubted who He was. He was sure, always. Jesus never had a moment of introspection regarding His identity in His entire life. He never questioned who His Father was or why He was here. Though He lived in the daily onslaught of doubt and outside questions regarding His identity, He lived fully sure, absolutely secure—He was His Father's Son.

Understand that I am not suggesting Jesus never experienced feelings of insecurity. But the Bible clearly reveals He never entertained those feelings. He was sure.

Think about how amazing that is. From the moment of His birth there were questions regarding His true identity. Born of a virgin, His inception was miraculous. But to those who didn't have the benefit of the Scriptures—"Son of God" and "God with us"—His birth was seemingly scandalous, and even appeared shameful. Jesus was actually born into the crisis. Yet, from the very beginning, everything we read reveals He was sure in His identity.

We only have one story of Jesus's childhood. Luke 2:42 tells us that when Jesus was twelve, his family traveled to Jerusalem for a census. On the way home, Joseph and Mary discovered that Jesus was missing from their caravan. They returned to Jerusalem and, after three days of searching, found Jesus at the temple. When they asked Him where He'd been, He said, *"Didn't you know I had to be in My Father's house?"* (Luke 2:49). This, the one and only story of Jesus's youth, reveals that He was sure in His identity as the Son of God. He knew who He was.

Throughout His life, the religious teachers, entire towns, and government officials constantly challenged Jesus's identity. Even His disciples got in on the act a couple of times. From His birth to His death, Jesus lived perfectly in the crisis. Not once did He doubt. Not once did He become insecure in who He was. He lived barraged by unbelief while championing His Father and revealing what it looks like when a son or daughter is sure in his or her identity.

Finally, Jesus's identity is officially questioned. Standing in front of the Jewish leaders, He is asked, *"Are You the Son of God, then?"* (Luke 22:70 NASB).

And Jesus, knowing what lay ahead, knowing that He faced the devastation of sin and the brutality of the cross…Jesus, sure in His identity, said, *"Yes, I am."*

The fact is, if you look at the life of Jesus, you discover that everywhere He went, His identity was questioned and challenged. And all the while Jesus stood firm, secure in His Father's love. Jesus lived sure in the midst of the crisis and revealed to us how we too can become sure. It went something like this: "Look up and let go."

Discovering My Identity

All of us are here, drawn by Love, undone in the wonder.

If there is anything I have learned over the last thirty-something years, it's that the question of identity is not only the theme of Jesus's story; it's ours as well.

I would like to suggest that knowing our Father is the most important thing we will ever do. The discovery of our Father's nature transforms and empowers us to live as His sons and daughters. Jesus modeled this for us. He lived, died, and arose sure in His identity. And because He was sure in His, we can become sure in ours.

The next several chapters focus primarily on our heavenly Father's perfect love nature. I am convinced that this journey we are on, this story we are living, has its breath in that revelation. It is through encounters with our Father that we are empowered to become the full expression of His sons and daughters in the here and now.

Like Jesus, we can know our Dad and live as the evidence of His love. When we know our heavenly Father, we become transformed into good earthly fathers and mothers. We become good brothers and sisters, good neighbors, good coworkers, good sons and daughters. We become world changers, living in miraculous fashion, discovering the wonders of His measureless Kingdom in our daily lives.

While I may never get to eat s'mores with Bob this side of heaven, my heavenly Father has a nice fire already blazing with graham crackers, marshmallows, and dark chocolate, that's right, *dark* chocolate.

And coffee. And He's keen on my presence. What am I saying? I am learning how to discover my heavenly Father. I am learning how to live in a greater revelation of His love on a daily basis.

On my journey I have learned that the only way to truly know who I am is to always be looking up and letting go, my eyes on my Father and my heart surrendered to Him. You see, my identity is found in the heart of my heavenly Father, and the only way I can know who I am is to encounter His love over and over and over again.

The point of all this is so that we can say, like Jesus, "If you have seen me, you have seen my Father." What an amazing statement!

An Identity Book

I stood on the edge to see what I could see,
I saw sons enraptured in the song of
Your love, in the fires of glory.

So when I told my friend who works in the publishing industry that I wasn't going to write a book on identity but rather a book about living in an intimate revelation of the Father's always-good love for us, I may have fibbed just a little. This is most definitely an "identity book."

Don't tell her, though.

But I think she already knows. She knows I am on a beautiful journey toward becoming sure. I am beginning to get better at seeing and encountering my heavenly Father's heart. I am learning how to live *in* my Father and know that He lives *in* me.

I am convinced that's why I exist: to encounter my Father's love, grow sure, and become His revelation to others. I am convinced it's why you exist as well, that you and I can say, like Jesus, "If you've seen me, you've seen my Father."

But it's a journey, a growing trust in His always-good love, a developing of revelation regarding the perfection of His goodness. I think we are all in different stages of looking up and letting go because we know, deep down inside, that's the only way to live.

Note

1.   For more information about this band, please visit http://www .bandofathousand.com.

Chapter Five

THE GOOD FATHER

The Prodigal Son, for Now...

I was sitting Indian style on the carpet in the living room in front of a three-foot stereo speaker. The song sent shivers down my spine. I was nine years old and obsessed. I would often sit for hours. I wasn't pretending to play the piano on the carpeted floor in our family room, I was playing the piano, and it was beautiful. The stereo speaker I sat in front of wasn't a speaker; it was the stage in front of a packed arena of worshipers. I played till my fingers bled. Well, maybe not until they bled. But I played so long and with such enthusiasm that my mom would occasionally come into the room and move the speaker so the carpet would wear evenly.

It was a powerful melody that Keith Green and I played together. The song was a retelling of the story about a father with two sons. It can be found in Luke 15, but if you ever get the chance, you've got to hear how Keith and I performed it. It was truly spectacular!

Have you ever heard the story?

A father has two sons. One day the younger son comes to his dad and asks for his inheritance. Dad doesn't balk; he simply gives his son some money. So the younger son goes out into the world where he foolishly spends his cash in every self-centered way conceivable. Eventually he runs out. Around that time the country goes into a depression and the only job he can find is feeding pigs.

Soon he realizes that the pigs are eating better than he is. That's when he decides to go home, beg forgiveness, and ask his father for a place among the servants.

Here is how Keith put it from the son's perspective.

> *I was near home, in sight of the house,*
> *My father just stared, dropped open his mouth,*
> *He ran up the road, and fell to my feet, and cried, and cried...*
> *"Father I've sinned, Heaven ashamed,*
> *I'm no longer worthy to wear your name,*
> *I've learned that my home is right where you are,*
> *Oh Father, take me in."[1]*

Then the story takes a wonderful turn. Keith and I captured it sweetly, his fingers passionately possessing the keys of his grand piano as my equally impassioned fingers sank deep into the carpet.

The father responded:

> *Bring the best robe, put it on my son,*
> *Shoes for his feet, hurry put them on.*
> *This is my son who I thought had died.*
> *Prepare a feast for my son's alive!*

This is where Keith and I would completely surrender to the life-giving spirit of the song. With his fingers and mine perfectly synced, I'd lend my inspired voice to his as we sang from the father's perspective. The rest of the band joining in, bringing the song to a crescendo...the horns, the strings...it was powerful!

> *My son was lost, oh thank You God he's found.*
> *My son was dead and he's now alive,*
> *Prepare a feast for my son's alive!*

It was a sweeping masterpiece—both the story and Keith's and my rendition of it. It was worship, pure and sweet.

After the last note had ceased to resonate in the cavity of my chest, Keith and I would head out and grab a hot chocolate. He usually got a larger one and I would get marshmallows in mine. We were tired, but it was the good kind of tired. We had given our all and yet somehow, if asked, we knew we had more to give.

As I've grown, so has my fantasy life. Hot chocolate has been replaced by coffee with an Irish kick and my company now includes Bono, Scott Crowder, Imogen Heap, and Bob Dylan. As to the story of the prodigal son, it has become more fascinating and revelatory. I now have a deeper understanding of why Keith loved it so much.

Keith's not alone. Everyone loves the prodigal son story. It's so right—a shattering display of the Father's love, a powerful example of mercy and grace. It's a story we can all relate to as we have all been prodigals in one way or another, we have all needed forgiveness, we have all needed a love that was bigger.

Our Inheritance

Come on in out of the cold, come home.

I imagine that when the fellas who translated the Bible came to the story of the prodigal son, there was a debate on what to title it. I imagine there was much prayer and dialogue that ran late into the night. Coffee was brewed, biscotti laid out, music heatedly discussed until they found consensus in Ray LaMontagne's "Till the Sun Turns Black." Finally they came to an agreement. Then the archbishop/apostle/leader guy stood, and, brushing the biscotti crumbs from his beard, he made his proclamation. Standing straight, shoulders back, chin up, and in a piercing nasal voice, he declared in high English, "Let this story heretofore be known as 'The Prodigal Son.'"

Yeah, I have no idea how it got it's title, but if I'd been there we would have listened to Bon Iver. But more to the point, I would have argued ardently and well that the story be titled, "The Good Father."

I am not saying they got it wrong, so please don't go telling everyone that Ray LaMontagne was a bad choice or that I think the Bible is flawed. I'm just saying I think that title is a little misleading as the story isn't fully about either of the sons but about the father.

The fact is that every story Jesus ever told was about a good father. Jesus's very existence, every breath He took, revealed *the* good Father.

I am convinced that our true inheritance as believers has nothing to do with money, land, or possessions of any kind. It's simply our Father's love revealed.

The younger son came home ready to beg for a place with the servants. Before he could even get to the front door, his dad is running out to meet him. Before he could even begin to say what he had probably rehearsed the whole way home, his dad is hugging and kissing and overwhelming him with affection.

I believe that it was at this moment that the younger son first truly saw his father as his dad; it was the first time the son discovered his father's true nature—love. And that is the moment he *actually* received his inheritance. Our inheritance is only available through a revelation of our Father's true nature. And our inheritance looks like, feels like, and in fact is intimacy.

The Ice Cream Sundae

"Hey, dude, there is something wrong with the ketchup. It tastes… different."

The four college students—two girls and two guys—had poured the ketchup all over their cheese fries.

"I'm sorry about that. Let me get you some new fries and a new bottle of ketchup."

I started to pick up the plate of fries when one of the guys said, "Dude, try one and see what I mean."

I didn't want to try their french fries. "That's all right," I said. "I will just get you some new fries." Then one of the girls jumped in, "It might just be us. You don't have to get us more. Try one."

It was an unusual request. It was also the end of a long day and a longer weekend. I was tired; I wasn't on my game. I tried one. It tasted fine and I said so. But I let them know that I would go and order them some new cheese fries anyway.

After dropping off the new fries, the bartender, who had seen the whole interaction, called me over. "Dude, as soon as you walked away from the table, they started laughing. I think they put something disgusting in the ketchup you ate."

I would like to tell you that I was very much like Jesus and that I graciously turned the other cheek, but that would be a lie. To be honest, I became dizzy with rage. "What could it have been?" My mind was spinning and coming up with several disgusting options. The more I thought about it, the angrier I became.

I spent the next ten minutes trying to think up retribution that didn't include jail time. Then, as I was walking by, they called me over. They were all laughing and smirking but I put on my nice waiter face and said, "What can I get for you?" They ended up ordering this particular restaurant's version of an ice cream sundae.

As I walked away, I admit it, I snapped.

Finding a rather private area next to the freezer, I fixed them a very special sundae. I thoroughly licked all four spoons and then, for good measure, I drizzled a little of my saliva into the sundae before adding the whipped cream and cherry. I walked it out, dropped it off, and in my kindest and most sincere waiter voice, said, "Enjoy, guys!"

A couple of minutes later I dropped off the check and saw that the sundae was gone and all four spoons appeared to have been used. With a sickening smile and in my best Hannibal Lector voice, I asked, "Did you all enjoy the sundae?

"Yeah, it was fine," one of the guys said, looking at me like I'd gone mad.

I continued. "Did you *all* have some?"

"What?" one of the girls asked.

I leaned in and asked again, "Did everyone eat it?" This time there was no missing my perverse smirk.

"Yes," she said, with a confused and slightly disturbed look on her face. The first hints of panic were showing on the faces of the others as well.

Then, one by one, I looked them in the eye. Finally, I grinned and said, "Good."

What We Believe

What we believe determines how we live. What we believe controls our thoughts, our emotions, and our actions. What's crazy is that we don't even need to have all the facts. We live by what we perceive to be the truth.

When it comes to our heavenly Father, I think it's astounding how greatly our lives are determined by what we believe. If we believe our Father is love and His love is perfected in His goodness, then we will trust Him. We will live in the expectation of a fuller, more powerful life. Our days will be marked by hope and joy and peace, even when life is hard, sad, and violent. If we believe that His love settles every need and answers every question that aches in our hearts, then we will step out boldly and risk. Our lives will be marked by love and the dangerous favor of God. We will be radical responders, living in a greater revelation of our Dad's love.

That said, if we are unsure regarding our Father's good love, then we'll find ourselves living on defense; our days will be marked by fear. Trust, hope, and joy will be fleeting; they will become principles that are impossible to maintain. In the good days we will be anxious, always waiting for the "other shoe to drop." We will try our hardest but we will live defensive and life will become a reaction to perceived attacks. And along the way, we may even spit in someone's ice cream sundae.

Jesus Didn't Come to Defend a Gospel

The story about the father with the prodigal son, the one I would have titled "The Good Father," that story doesn't end with the reconciliation of the younger son. Remember, this father had two sons.

> Meanwhile, the older son was in the field. When he came near the house, he heard music and dancing. So he called one of the servants and asked him what was going on. "Your brother has come," he replied, "and your father has killed the fattened calf because he has him back safe and sound."
>
> The older brother became angry and refused to go in. So his father went out and pleaded with him. But he answered his father, "Look! All these years I've been slaving for you and never disobeyed your orders. Yet you never gave me even a young goat so I could celebrate with my friends. But when this son of yours who has squandered your property with prostitutes comes home, you kill the fattened calf for him!"
>
> "My son," the father said, "you are always with me, and everything I have is yours" (Luke 15:25-31).

So the older son comes in from working out in the field to find a celebration party well underway for his prodigal brother's return. He is upset and will not go into the house to join the party. When his father comes out to meet him, we learn that the older son's perception of reality has greatly affected how he has lived his life. He tells his dad he's been *"slaving out in the fields"* for him. He was essentially saying,

"Why on earth are you celebrating my brother? What's he done for you lately?"

The father's response is absolutely over the top because it describes our inheritance: "Son, why would you be out slaving for me. Everything I have is yours. All that I am is available to you, no slaving required. You have access to it simply because you are my son" (Luke 15:31 paraphrase).

The older son's frustrated interaction with his dad reveals that, just like his younger brother, he didn't truly know his father's love nature. Therefore, he had no access to his true inheritance as a son. Because his perception of life was determined by a lie, he slaved in a works-based reality for a harsh master instead of colaboring in a relational, intimate revelation of his dad's love.

It's quite possible and, in fact, likely that this fella would have spit in his brother's ice cream given the chance. Heck, he might have even spit in his dad's ice cream—just saying. It's easy to become offended when you are not living in a daily revelation of love.

What's scary to me is that when we can't see God as a good Father, we not only miss out on our inheritance, but we actually find ourselves sided against Him. When we slave, we are unable to celebrate mercy or grace in the lives of others. The scary thing about slaving, besides the fact that it sucks, is that it will actually position us against the very Father we think we serve.

There are a lot of older brother rumblings coming from the church today—religious slaves seeking judgment for failed, lost, deceived, and even restored prodigals. In fact, I would guess much of the world sees the church as the older brother, slaving for a Father while wagging our finger in judgment at a lost, lonely, broken, and confused world.

Here's what I believe: the desire to see judgment come to a lost sinner, a fallen, or even a deceived saint, is not the heart of the Father—ever.

I was in a conversation with a friend the other day and essentially said just that. He challenged me with, "So are you saying we shouldn't confront and expose lies and immorality?"

"Only if we can do it without taking our eyes off Dad (Love)," I said.

When we take our eyes off our Father and His perfect love for us, we forget why we are here. We become more interested in defending a set of principles than revealing love. Jesus didn't come to defend a gospel; He came to reveal the perfection of our Father's love. It's religious vanity to think we are here to do anything different.

I have met many Christians and even read a few books that would rather focus on the problem instead of the answer, the *need* instead of *love*. I have heard many messages that exploit need instead of reveal love. Sadly, much of the church is spitting in the ice cream sundae of their brother and their neighbor, and and calling it Christianity. God doesn't want to be defended but He loves to be revealed.

Allow me to repeat: Jesus wasn't concerned with defending a gospel. He was too busy *revealing* the Gospel—His Father's always-good love. He lived miraculously, died selflessly, and rose powerfully, all so we might be restored back to our place in the family—as sons and daughters of God. All so we might have full access to our inheritance—the love nature of our Father.

If we don't know our Dad, we are forced to live in the insecurity of slavery, under the weight of need, and we are compelled to defend a gospel. If we don't know our Father's love, then, like the older brother, we will find ourselves in direct opposition to our Dad. And you know what direct opposition looks like? Judgment.

God, forgive us for judging when we were created to love.

I don't need to defend the faith to know who I am. Neither my identity nor my value is discovered in my beliefs, it's discovered in my Father's nature. It's discovered in how He sees me—I am loved.

A Good Master and a Greater Revelation

This book is not a campaign against the idea that we are not to know God as a good Master; it's simply an invitation to come to our senses.

> *When he came to his senses, he said, "How many of my father's hired men have food to spare, and here I am starving to death! I will set out and go back to my father and say to him: Father, I have sinned against heaven and against you. I am no longer worthy to be called your son; make me like one of your hired men"* (Luke 15:17-19).

The prodigal son comes home because he knows his dad is a better master than the world he has been slaving for. While the younger son never truly knew his good father, he did know him as a good master. That limited perspective was powerful enough to invite a despairing son back home after he had desperately failed.

A good master can draw the prodigal home, but only a good father can empower a son. Jesus wasn't telling us this story so we could know the good Master; He was revealing the good Father to us. Why? Because a good Master can still be slaved for, and slavery is never our Father's heart for us.

If our revelation of God as a good Master doesn't mature into a revelation of God as a good Father, we will find ourselves enslaved either to the world or religion. The truth that God is a good Master is a wonderful starting place, but was never meant to be the destination. The journey of knowing God as more than a good Master is filled with exponential life, exponential righteousness, peace, joy, trust, power, and authority. When we know the good Father, we live in the inheritance of sons and daughters, the measureless love of heaven.

Everything He Has Is Ours

I turn my face to a blazing Son,
Your glory falls, Your Kingdom comes.

The moment the younger son truly saw his father's nature is the moment he received his inheritance. And it's the same for us. The moment we see Dad, we are set free and empowered to be His sons and daughters, and that's where our inheritance is accessed. Our Father's perfect love nature revealed is our inheritance, and this is how we are created to live—in the power and authority of the same love that Jesus lived.

Jesus told us this story to reveal His Father—period! He told this story so that we might live beyond the title of "slave" and grow in the freedom, power, and authority of our true inheritance, as His sons and daughters.

When I was nine years old, running my fingers along the ivory carpet keys alongside Keith Green, I was (dare I say it) brilliant. My every finger stroke matched Keith's. I would close my eyes, throw back my head, and sing with him, sometimes harmonizing, sometimes taking over completely. We were phenomenal together. I knew it and he knew it. It didn't matter that I couldn't play the piano.

What we believe determines how we live. Looking back, those days on the carpet were instrumental in my pursuit of worship in the form of melody, harmony, and rhythm. What I believed as a child determined not just how I lived, but who I have become.

Just so, when we see God as our Father and become sure in His love, we are transformed, giving us access to our destiny. When we see our Father and become sure in His love, all impossibilities become possibilities—it's called heaven on earth.

Greater Works—Why Not Now?

We'll take the hill, me and the thunder sons,
We won't quit till Thy Kingdom comes.

Just before Jesus ascended to heaven, He told us that we could live a life like His. In fact, He said we could experience even greater works than those He experienced (see John 14:12). It wasn't a suggestion; it was a prophetic proclamation. Jesus looked into the future and saw sons and daughters living in their inheritance. He saw "greater works" believers.

Why not now?

Some have told me that the "greater works" life Jesus described is for the last days and a coming generation. Well, I would like to suggest that we are living in the last days and we are the coming generation. Honestly, I believe it is my responsibility as a son of God to pursue a revelation of His always-good love that empowers me to live the "greater works" life Jesus promised.

He said, "Everything I have is yours." What's it look like if we started believing Him?

Could it be that we are called to pray powerful prayers? Could it be that we are destined to live miraculous lives? What if we prayed and lived in such a way that entire families discovered the love of Jesus? What if we knew our Father's love so profoundly that neighbors and coworkers experienced healing in their bodies and favor in their relationships? What if we so believed His love that our marriages became beacons of hope for a faithless world? What if our encounters with God were so evident that our kids became firebrands for the King? What if the greater works He promised really were available to us here and now?

I am absolutely convinced that we have not yet seen on this earth the full wonders of love. Love received is only fully realized when it is given away. I believe our Father is raising up radical sons and daughters who will live in their inheritance and love with authority and power, sons and daughters who will live believing that everything He has is ours!

Note

1. "The Prodigal Son Suite" was written and performed by Keith Green.

Chapter Six

THE MEXICAN HAMBURGER

The Rabbit

I know Your story, all the glory,
It's a truth that defines and begins.

I had already used every trick I knew to fight sleep. It was strange because I'd endured much longer trips with less fatigue, but this one was different. I couldn't concentrate; all I wanted to do was close my eyes.

At one point I almost pulled over to ask Karen if she would take the wheel but thought, "If I'm this tired, she must be as well." So I soldiered on. We were driving on a straight stretch of highway through flat farmland when I saw it. It was sitting out in the field, just off to the right. It was staring right at me.

It was a rabbit. But this was no ordinary rabbit. This one was three stories high and about half a football field long. And it was bright neon pink. And it was made out of marshmallow. It reminded me of a Peeps—those marshmallow candies that are sold during the Easter season.

At first I was awed by the sheer size of it. But my awe quickly became terror as it hopped once, twice, and then landed directly on the road in front of our speeding car. I jerked the steering wheel violently, fishtailing the car onto the right shoulder while simultaneously slamming my breaks, bringing us to a skidding halt.

A semitruck flew past, horn raging, as Karen woke screaming.

"Jason!...What happened?"

I shook my head and rubbed my eyes. The rabbit just sat there, in the middle of the road, watching me.

"What is it?" Karen demanded this time. "Did we get a flat? Are you okay?...Jason!"

I couldn't take my eyes off of it. It didn't like me. I could feel it in my bones.

Karen was yelling now. "Jason! What's going on?"

Without taking my glazed eyes off of the neon monster, I mumbled, "A giant pink Peeps bunny just jumped on the road in front of us."

"What?"

"I think you better drive," I said. It was the last lucid thought I had for three days.

Bad Hamburguesa

Karen had to be as exhausted as I was. We had flown all night from Mexico City. Our flights had been substantially lower in cost if we flew into Toronto, so even though it was a three-hour drive from where we lived in Rochester, New York, that's what we did. She was sleeping in the front seat next to me while I sped us toward our cozy, 400-square-foot apartment.

It had been an amazing missions trip and we were ready to be home and snuggle in a real bed together. We were newly married and had spent a week sleeping in separate tents because the missionaries leading the trip were apparently from the 1800s and "we didn't want to give any appearance of impropriety"—whatever that means.

"How do you think it became known as the missionary position?" I'd asked. Nobody laughed. But I didn't want to sleep with my wife so we could practice being good missionaries; I wanted to sleep with my wife because it was cold!

We spent a week up in the hills of a small Mexican village. During the day the weather was a perfect sixty-five degrees and sunny; at night it felt like it was minus fifty. Karen slept in the women's tent; I slept in the men's. We spent our nights dressed in every article of clothing we had, but we still found ourselves freezing in our flimsy sleeping bags, all alone.

Well, not alone, just not together. I tried snuggling with the doctor missionary next to me, but it was a little awkward. We didn't know each other that well. And he had heard my joke.

It was a medical missions trip. Seeing as neither Karen nor I had any credentials in that department, we spent our days in practical service and prayer. Karen played a large role in preparing our food with the local women. We had a great time with the name of each meal as every one of them had the same ingredients—tortillas and beans. So we had tortilla pancakes for breakfast, with beans! Tortilla sandwiches for lunch, with beans! And tortilla hamburgers for dinner, with beans!

At the end of our week we hugged new friends, we traded mailing addresses, and then caught a bus back to Mexico City for our flight home. Needless to say, we were all ready for some flavor. We had just enough time to enjoy a Mexico City restaurant. The missionary leading the trip took us to one of his favorite spots before we headed to the airport. The menu was in Spanish, but it's pretty obvious if you're looking for it—*hamburguesa*. It had been haunting my cold, lonely dreams for a week. Now I could finally put it to rest—*hamburguesa*!

I'm not a complete idiot. I knew you couldn't just eat anything in Mexico City. So I asked our trusty leader if he thought the hamburgers were safe to eat. He shrugged, "Yeah, they should be fine." So on that glowing endorsement, I ordered a *hamburguesa*.

It didn't taste right. I ate it anyway. Why? Cause it wasn't tortillas and beans, I guess. Plus, I'd never had a Mexican hamburger before; maybe that's just the way they taste.

We caught taxis to the airport and after several hours waiting on the tarmac because of "mechanical difficulties," we finally headed for home.

As I already mentioned, it was an all-night flight in which neither my new bride or myself could sleep. We arrived in Canada absolutely exhausted. We said our good-byes to everyone we had missionary-*ed* with, then we caught a shuttle to our car and finally began the three-hour drive home.

Though I wasn't feeling well, I told Karen I would drive. It's what new husbands do. She let me, because that's what new wives do. It was about 8:30 in the morning and I had driven maybe an hour. Karen had immediately fallen asleep. I was dizzy, bleary-eyed, and at my weakest.

And that's when the rabbit made his move.

I have no memory of the rest of the drive home or the three days of delirium that followed. Apparently, they were extremely uncomfortable for both Karen and myself.

I know what you're thinking, "How is Jason going to tie this story into a deep, profound spiritual revelation?" Maybe I won't. Maybe I just wanted to warn you that if the *hamburguesa* you are eating doesn't taste right, it's probably bad *hamburguesa*, and for goodness' sake, stop eating it!

The Skilsaw

For most of my life, I have been fed a lie. For most of my life, even though the lie hasn't tasted right, I have swallowed it down anyway. And worse, I have even fed it to others.

There were a couple of years when my family lived in western New York. We had a house on Cedar Street, which was located just a few blocks from the church school we attended. At that time I was around eleven years old, my sister Aimee was ten, and my brother Joel was eight. We often walked to and from school, and had many adventures along the way.

Coming home from school one day, we discovered not only Mom's car but also Dad's truck in the driveway. Dad's truck was never in the driveway before 5:00 p.m. We ran into the house, excitedly looking for him. Mom met us at the door. Dad had been in an accident.

My dad had a construction company at the time and had been on a jobsite. Apparently, while cutting a two-by-four, the Skilsaw snagged on the wood, bounced out of his right hand, and landed on the left. Then the saw proceeded to crawl up his arm. He had several deep gashes. The worst was his thumb, which he almost severed.

I walked into the bedroom with my brother and sister. Dad was in bed, his hand bandaged. He had been sleeping but was now awake and sitting up. He smiled at us. Then he showed us his bandages and told us how it happened, and how he should have been more careful, and how the doctors barely saved his thumb. Yes, it hurt, but he had medicine now and felt better. Yes, lots of blood...

When my dad finished explaining the accident, my brother and sister's interest waned. Not mine. I moved to the next (at least to me) obvious question. "Why did it happen?" I asked. I didn't just want to know how; I had to know why. As a kid, "why" was one of my favorite questions. It still seems to come up from time to time.

I put my dad in some tough situations with that question as a kid. "Dad, why did God let Keith Green die?" "Dad, why does God let African children go hungry" And finally, "Dad, why do you think God nearly let you cut your thumb off?"

My dad would have a completely different answer to that question if it were asked today. But at the time, my dad had been fed bad *hamburguesa*, a lie. And it caused him to see and say things that weren't true, so he responded, "I think God may be trying to get my attention."

It was a lie. But at the time, my dad believed it, and so did I. It's not that I made an intentional theological decision regarding the nature of God, but more that I was eleven and my subconscious bought into it. The idea that my heavenly Father uses Skilsaws, that He either orchestrates or just allows bad things to happen to people so He might get their attention, or teach them a lesson, or to get them to do His will—it became a part of my spiritual DNA.

Guess what? It's bad *hamburguesa*; and if you eat it, you'll get sick. It's a lie that is as old as humankind. It's a lie that was birthed in the Garden of Eden. Every day, both believers and unbelievers buy into it. Like me, they swallow it down and then pass it along. In my opinion, it's the worst kind of lie. It's the worst because it distorts the true nature of our heavenly Father. It implies that God is about control.

Self-Control

Told my heart to never forget, Your Spirit birthed in me.

Several years ago Ethan and I had a talk. It was shortly after he had briefly forgotten how his heavenly Father saw him, and in that moment he said some things to his mom he didn't truly believe. I met him in his room.

There are nine fruits of the Spirit, they are found in Galatians (see 5:22-23), but Ethan was only aware of one fruit. It was the fruit that Mom and Dad had been going on about for months—self-control.

"Ethan, I don't want to control you. The fact is, I can't control you." I smiled at him. He was following me. We were in familiar territory.

I was about to remind him of the importance of self-control when I said something that surprised us both.

"Son, God doesn't want to control you either. Control is counter to who He is. But God does want you to control yourself."

It just came out of my mouth. And while it sounded wrong to my ears, my heart leapt in my chest. I knew the statement to be true.

It's a paradox: "a proposition that seems self-contradictory or absurd but in reality expresses a possible truth."[1]

Ethan looked at me confused, which is the proper response when being confronted with a paradox.

I continued, "Control is the opposite of who God is. God is always about freedom. Did you know that?"

Ethan nodded. It wasn't the first time he's heard me say that.

"Son, only you have control of your heart and that's the way God wants it."

For the next half an hour my son and I talked about the wonder of the Holy Spirit, the same Holy Spirit who lived in Jesus, enabling Him to live righteous when tempted to sin; the same Holy Spirit who empowered Him to a miraculous life, who was with Him through His death, who raised Him and seated Him at the right hand of the Father, who gave Him all authority; the same brilliant Holy Spirit who lives in Ethan and me. And one of the evidences of His indwelling, one of the fruits of His infilling presence, is self-control (see Gal. 5:22-23).

After talking, Ethan and I wrestled for a couple minutes; I know the language of his love. And then I went to the kitchen, poured fresh coffee into my favorite faded blue mug, a gift from my good friend Carver, sat at our old oak plank farm table with my Mac, put my headphones on, listening to John Mark McMillan, and began to write...

I believe self-control is the only kind of control God endorses. It's the gift of choice and the evidence of His Spirit within us. It's why there were two trees in the Garden. Adam and Eve had the freedom to choose, to trust or distrust. God gave control of Adam to Adam and control of Eve to Eve. Self-control was the evidence that they were walking in freedom. It was the fruit of the Holy Spirit reigning in them.

The lie that separated humanity from God in the Garden was a lie of control—who had it? The fact is, Adam and Eve were walking out the perfection of their freedom through the gift of self-control.

Then Satan shows up and distorts the nature of God with a lie. The lie? God is trying to control you. And they bought it. They believed that God was withholding some part of Himself and therefore some measure of freedom from them. And to this day that lie continues to enslave.

The root of Satan's lie was that God is about control, that God wants to control us. And it's a huge lie! The idea that He would withhold some aspect of His nature suggests an imperfection in our Father's love. I believe this original distortion of our Father's nature is still the foundational lie that separates us from His love and the fullness of our freedom and authority in Christ.

The fact is, Adam and Eve sold their self-control, and with it their freedom, to Satan. And until Jesus arrived, humanity lived in that paradigm, enslaved to sin where once they were perfect expressions of God's love. Then Jesus came. He lived, He died, and He rose. He took all authority and He gave it back to us, and with it He gave us back self-control. Through the cross and in the power of the Holy Spirit, we now have the freedom to control ourselves again!

I could control Ethan's behavior, I could force, manipulate, or straight up shame him into obedience. I could make him behave. But someday my boy will be a man and beyond my ability to control. And God forgive me if I haven't empowered him to control himself. Control is always focused on behavior. But love reveals identity. Control will enslave you to need, where love will reveal your identity and empower you to live free.

As a good father, I am less interested in behavior and more interested in identity. That is to say, I want my boy to know love and, in love's freedom, control himself. If Ethan knows my love, and more, our Father's love, he is set free and empowered to be a son of the King. And in that identity and in the power of the Holy Spirit, he can control himself—behavior follows identity.

While I can for a time control Ethan's actions, I can't truly control Ethan's heart, nor do I want to. Neither does God want to control our hearts. Isn't that a radical thought? He doesn't want to control us. He is never about control; He can't stand it. His love is the perfection of His goodness and it's always about freedom. And freedom looks like sons and daughters living powerfully in control of themselves and in all the authority of His love.

I think this lie that God is about control is a big one—I am going after it hard. Anywhere in my life where I find it, I am surrendering to His perfect love.

God Does Not Want to Control Us

If the truth sets us free, then a lie shackles us. The lie that God wants to control us can make us horribly sick. It can turn sons and daughters into slaves and slaves into fanatic religious dictators.

When we believe that God is about control, we are forced to believe things that aren't true and see things that aren't real. That's what happened to me. I walked around for years subtly believing that the flu was the response to some sin in my life. When my car was broken into, God let it happen to help me refocus on the disciplines of my faith. When I didn't get the job I wanted and needed, it probably was because I didn't love God enough. If the furnace broke in my home, God may have instigated it so I could learn how to trust Him with my finances. Or maybe He was disciplining me because of my poor financial planning. Essentially, life's hardships were sent or allowed by my Father to teach me how to live better, stay disciplined, and love Him more.

It's not that I didn't see and experience the goodness of God through life's journey. It's just that the power of His goodness was sadly reduced to the limits enforced by the lie that existed in my heart about His nature. I was enslaved to the lie that my heavenly Father was a controlling bipolar deity—one day full of love, the next wielding a Skilsaw. So I lived insecure in my relationship with Him, never sure what was next.

Whether saved or unsaved, what we believe about the nature of God determines how we relate with Him and directly affects our freedom. When we believe that our Father is about control, then when something goes wrong, someone has to be blamed. If we are believers, then for the most part, we blame others or ourselves. For unbelievers it's a little easier to blame God. But the bottom line is that if we believe God is about control, then when everything goes south, He ultimately gets the blame.

The news calls natural disasters "acts of God." And sadly, much of the church still teaches that the city struck by a disaster had it coming due to its sin. In the wake of a natural disaster, we hear every conceivable misrepresentation of God's nature. What makes me sick is to hear it from the church. It reveals that we agree with the world's assessment of a petty, controlling God who has us like puppets on a string.

Believing God wants to control us affects everything. Every experience and encounter is filtered through the insecurity of our relationship with a small God. A control-based perspective of God is evidenced from the subtle anxiety we experience in our heart when the furnace breaks down to the blatant sense of righteousness we feel when a rapist gets the death penalty. A control-based perspective of God forces us to say, "They had it coming." Control births blame and someone has to pay.

Truth Is...

It's a truth that defines and begins.

Truth is, someone has to pay. Truth is, He already did.

It's only been in the last ten years or so that I have begun to realize with growing amazement and thankfulness that God isn't about control. Quite the opposite; He is about authority. He has all authority. That's what Jesus said in my Bible: *"All authority in heaven and on earth has been given to Me"* (Matt. 28:18).

Jesus didn't come, live here with us, die for us, and rise again so He could be in control. He came to repossess for us and then give back to us authority. Control and authority are two entirely different things; control operates in the reality of need while authority is about love.

My Bible also says that it was for freedom that Jesus set me free (see Gal. 5:1). While control enslaves, authority sets me free. My heavenly Father has been absolutely amazing at working His freedom in me. As He's revealed His love—His presence and His goodness—I've begun to discover that His love conflicted greatly with the lie buried ever so deep in my soul. His love is always bigger than the lie.

I am daily, by faith, choosing to believe a radical truth about the nature of God. This truth has changed everything. The truth? God is love and His love is always good—always. That's my theology.

Goodness is not a sometimes deal with God. Goodness is an extension of His nature, of His love. It's not a theory or a concept; it's an absolute, a greater revelation. It's a truth we can either believe fully or not at all. Our heavenly Father is fully, completely good, all the time. And if we can learn to believe this, we have found the core value by which everything in life is measured. Life is about knowing His good love and then knowing more; it's about becoming sure.

He Values Our Thumbs

I'm overwhelmed in the wonder of You,
I count it all joy, cause You're always good.

I have scanned my memory and talked in-depth with my siblings. In my thorough investigation, I am confident in this next statement being absolutely, one hundred percent true. My dad never used a Skilsaw on any of us to get our attention or to teach us a lesson. In fact, I am sure it never even crossed his mind. Now I realize my dad is one of the top five dads in world history, but even if he were just an average dad, I am confident the Skilsaw would never have entered the equation.

If my dad wants to get my attention, he calls me by my name—the one he gave me. If he wants to teach me something, he demonstrates it to me by how he lives. If he wants to impart to me knowledge, he reveals his heart through his words and acts of love. He's always wanted the best for me, and to this day he places a high value on my thumbs.

My dad loves me. He has always been there for me. He supports me, encourages me, and lifts me up in prayer. He gave me a home full of love; he provided for me and cheered me on in all of my pursuits. He came to my hockey games, took me camping, dreamed with me about music, and encouraged me in business, in writing, and in ministry.

But if I told you that there was one time he nearly cut my thumb off in order to get my attention, what would you think about my dad? You'd doubt the ninety-nine good stories because of the one involving a Skilsaw, wouldn't you? You would doubt his goodness. Maybe not entirely, but a seed of doubt would enter your mind, and from small seeds big trees sometimes grow.

I believe there is a great shift that takes place in our hearts the day we decide to agree with the truth that our heavenly Father is always good, that His love is perfected in His goodness, and that it is impossible for a good Father to use Skilsaws on his kids. When we see our

Father as He truly is, we are free to discover the authority of His love and to become sure in His love, secure in His goodness. Our authority is found when we see the true nature of our heavenly Father and then choose to both agree and align our hearts in that revelation.

Stop Eating It

Believing a lie about our Father's love enslaves us to a dull, striving, impotent existence. It's bad *hamburguesa*. It distorts reality. For goodness' sake, stop eating it!

The fact is, I can't know who I am until I know my Father. And if I am misguided regarding His nature, I live unsure regarding mine. If I relate to Him like He has love in one hand and a Skilsaw in the other, I live insecure, enslaved to a controlling tyrant. If I believe my Father instigates or blesses the use of Skilsaws, then the truth of my identity as His son is greatly limited to my misunderstanding of His nature. If I believe I am to slave for Him, then my freedom as a son or daughter is greatly hindered.

I once heard a great analogy that best describes this kind of slavery. Let's say I have a million dollars in my bank account but I'm only aware of a thousand. If that's the case, then I will live in the limitation of the thousand. Every decision I make will be restricted to the lie that I only have a thousand bucks. My needs will go unmet, my family's needs will go unmet, and giving becomes virtually nonexistent. I live broke and powerless.

If I don't know the truth, I become a slave to the lie. If I believe my heavenly Father is not always good, that sometimes He allows bad things to happen to people to get their attention, then I live enslaved to that lie. Therefore, when someone is sick, I can't pray with faith, authority, and power because maybe God is allowing the sickness. When someone is broke, I have to make sure it isn't God's will before giving. When someone is emotionally bound, I am forced to check in with God before setting him or her free. To be honest, if my heavenly Father is not always good, then I don't want any part of Him.

Note

1. "Paradox," from Dictionary.com, http://dictionary.reference.com/browse/paradox?s=t, accessed July 16, 2013.

Chapter Seven

THE OSCILLATING GOD

The Oscillating God

I'm overwhelmed in the wonder of You,
I count it all joy cause You're always good.

I lay in my homemade sleeping bag, a queen-size sheet that Karen had halved and sown at the bottom. I stared at the ceiling perspiring from every pore, soaking through my thin sheet. My sweaty head lay on a rolled T-shirt, a backpacker's pillow. The stifling heat caused my breathing to come in gasps. Every minute or so I would squeeze my eyes shut to clear the pooled sweat gathering at the corners. Both the sweat and the mosquito netting that hung from an exposed beam just above my head meant my vision was a constant blur.

I lay in my cocoon, trying not to move, and observed the mosquitoes trapped inside the netting. I realized that even with mosquitoes, the old adage is true: the proverbial grass is always greener on the other side. The handful of mosquitoes that shared my living space were lethargically trying to escape while a thousand others outside the netting were frantic to get in. Of course, my little roommates were only trying to leave because they were too drunk to continue the feast and were seeking a safe place to sleep it off.

I was thankful for my shabby netting—it seemed to work well enough, at least regarding the mosquitoes. I doubted it would stop the rats that ran across the exposed beams over my head. Fortunately, they seemed to have some place to go and were less interested in me than I in them.

The Philippines is the hottest, most humid place I have ever been in my life. New Orleans in July doesn't hold a candle to its suffocating heat. It was unworldly, unrelenting. I was eight days into a thirteen-day whirlwind worship mission trip with a handful of saints. There were five of us in total lying on the second floor of the two-story tin shack located on the side of a Filipino volcano. That's right, in case the natural heat wasn't enough, we were on the side of an active burner. We had poured our hearts out all day and we were beyond exhausted, but none of us could sleep. Our insomnia wasn't the result of the disagreeable plywood floor, the ravenous mosquitoes, or the indisposed rats, it was because of the infuriating beautiful oscillating fan.

That fan was the center of our universe; it was my delight and my torment. It was life and death. For the brief seconds the moving air brushed my clammy skin I knew to the core of my being that God was good and He loved me. "Oh, God," I blissfully sighed. And then the stupid thing moved on and I began to doubt. "Oh, God," I cried out again, this time with notes of desperation.

I don't know about you, but much of my life I have served an oscillating God, much like that fan. You know, my delight one day, my torture the next, the guy that has sunshine and ponies in one hand and Thor's hammer in the other. I have determined His nature through the lens of my needs. When life was kind, with demands met, health great, and friendships deep and true, I'd sigh blissfully, "Oh, God."

But life isn't always kind. The hammer drops. And when the valley of the shadow of death is upon us, that's when we're challenged to believe that our Father's nature doesn't change. He isn't fickle. He hasn't gotten tired of us or had second thoughts about us. He hasn't turned His heart from us; He's not judging us or condemning us. He is still the same always-good love He has always been. But that can be a challenge.

I am growing in my revelation regarding my Father's heart toward me. "Only goodness and love all the days of my life," that's what I say. I say it when life is a mountaintop and I am learning to say it when life is a valley. Notice the word *learning*.

I am learning my Father doesn't oscillate. I am learning He will not turn His back on me. He is never my torture; He is only my delight! His love is steadfast and relentless. His love is pure and beautiful. His love pursues me, enraptures me, consumes me. His love is the beginning, the end, the before, the after, and everything in between. And I am learning this more and more, becoming surer.

The Father Never Turned His Back

Do you know there is only one time throughout the Gospels when Jesus refers to God in the first person? Every other time He referred to God as Father. But on the cross, in pain and carrying the weight of sin and death, He cried out, *"My God, My God, why have You forsaken Me?"* (Matt. 27:46).

It was a wail of absolute anguish, one that many have interpreted to mean that somehow Jesus was, if but for a moment, abandoned, left to Himself, even shunned by His Father. I have heard this moment described by many as God turning His back on Jesus. As if the Father oscillated. It baffles the mind to think that an always-good and loving Father would do this— leave His Son to carry the weight of sin and death alone, abandoned in His darkest moment.

But I believe the Father never turned His back, He never left or forsook Jesus, He never abandoned Him, not even for a moment. His love was just as good as it's always been. He did not oscillate.

"But a time is coming, and has come, when you will be scattered, each to his own home. You will leave Me all alone. Yet I am not alone, for My Father is with Me" (John 16:32). That is what Jesus told His disciples before going to the cross. That seems pretty clear, doesn't it? The Father wasn't going anywhere. But if that's true, what do we do with Jesus's anguished cry to God on the cross?

"My God, My God, why have You forsaken Me?" This is the pivotal Scripture that is used to suggest that somehow the Father turned His face from His Son.

Did you know this statement was an echo of Jesus's earthly forefather? Jesus was quoting the poet, King David, from Psalm 22:1. As Davidic psalms go, Psalm 22 is fairly standard. David wrestled through life's mountaintops and valleys with the raw authenticity that makes him an Old Testament favorite.

What's amazing is that several verses after, *"My God, my God, why have You forsaken me,"* David writes, *"He has not despised nor abhorred the affliction of the afflicted; nor has He hidden His face from him; but when he cried to Him for help, He heard"* (Ps. 22:24 NASB).

It's interesting to me that Jesus points us to a Scripture that ultimately determines that the Father doesn't hide His face or "turn His back." In fact, the truth is quite the opposite: *"but when He cried to Him for help, He heard…"*

The Father didn't oscillate. He did not oscillate. As the old hymn writer wrote: "There is no shadow of turning with Thee."[1]

The Nature of Soap

"Should I stick my hand in the toilet?" That was the question I asked myself. It was Jeremy's bar of soap. I had lost mine somewhere along the journey. It's not like I'd been aiming for the toilet; everyone knows soap is slippery. He'd understand if I told him what happened.

We were nearing the end of the whirlwind thirteen-day, three-island, two-conference, worship missions trip in the Philippines. Jeremy, one of my closest friends, was a part of the team. He is a good mate to have with you on these kinds of adventures, as he always brings enough toiletries to share, with me. Though I think his patience was wearing thin when I helped myself to his closely rationed Q-tips.

In case you think I was taking advantage, don't. I paid him back with beef jerky and Gold Bond powder. Honestly, I was surprised he hadn't thought to bring either.

We were in a small church building constructed of mismatched pieces of plywood, sheet metal, and cinder blocks. The little church crowded a narrow road on the side of a volcano and was hemmed in by other ramshackle buildings and farmers' fields, all surrounded by dense jungle.

The toilet was in the corner of a room downstairs. Two walls and a door, both constructed of paper-thin plywood, were all that separated it from daily life and offered only the appearance of privacy. The toilets I experienced in the Philippines were porcelain bowls, no water tank, no seats (which are apparently an American luxury). This toilet was no different. Also, like most Filipino toilets I'd encountered, it was connected to sewage but not running water.

Next to the toilet was a large barrel filled with clean*ish* water. Floating in the water was a big plastic cup. The cup was for both flushing and bathing. Oh, I forgot to note, the toilet room was also the shower.

I stood naked and skinny, trying not to touch the black mildewed flimsy walls. With the plastic cup, I poured water over my head, making sure to keep my eyes and mouth closed. I was fully lathered when Jeremy's soap determined to be unruly. It could have flown into the water barrel, but it didn't.

"Maybe he *wouldn't* understand," I thought nervously.

Jeremy's generosity was wearing thin, so I couldn't come back empty-handed. I made the hard decision. Naked, sudsed, bleary-eyed, and dry heaving, I plunged my hand into the murky water and retrieved the soap.

I believe soap is inherently clean. While its surface can get dirty, it's in soap's nature to be clean. So I lathered it, rinsed it, and returned it with a clean conscience. Jeremy was a little mad. But that was mostly because I waited until well after we had returned home to tell him about the incident. And also maybe because I had borrowed soap from one of the other fellas for the remainder of the trip.

Jeremy doesn't hold my view on soap. And apparently my view on soap isn't unwavering. After I told him what happened, he grinned, but it was not a nice grin. It was evil and promised malicious retribution.

You know that saying, "$@#! happens"? Well, because this is a book for Christians and no publisher will let me keep that word in the book, I thought I'd rephrase it using the story from the last chapter. Try this: "Skilsaws happen."

It's true. Sometimes it's because of carelessness, which wasn't the case with the soap (seriously, Jeremy, let it go…please). Sometimes Skilsaws happen because we miss God, we sin, we fall short. Sometimes Skilsaws happen because someone else messed up. Sometimes it just happens for no apparent reason. A bar of soap jumps out of your hand and into the toilet; a Skilsaw jumps out of your hand and nearly severs your thumb.

Sometimes while you follow God and live a life of faith, while you chase Him radically believing, while living the sincerest worship lifestyle ever known to man, your soap still ends up in the toilet. Sometimes Skilsaws happen and, when they do, the desperate cry that bursts from our hearts often sounds something like, *"My God, my God, why have You forsaken me?"*

But He hasn't. His love for us is still perfect. He does not oscillate.

Circumstances

It's the weight of my surrender that brought the mountain to its knees.

Several years ago Karen and I were assessing our finances and the fact that we were eleven months behind on our mortgage and two months behind on our utilities. We had less than ten dollars to our name, mostly in loose change, and we had about a gallon of gas in the van. Karen is amazing, her faith stunning. She is well acquainted with our Father's good love and made a statement that highlights it. "We have food in the fridge. We are blessed and God is so good."

"God is good." Sometimes it's the most powerful sentence in the universe, a statement of profound faith.

"God is good." It's true when we can pay our mortgage and when we can't.

Karen and I are learning that a need met can never be the measuring stick of our Father's goodness, it can only be the evidence. His goodness and His love will follow us all the days of our lives and will never be measured or determined by our circumstances. This faith is the foundational truth upon which everything else in our lives is built.

Karen and I have prayed when she starts to get a migraine: "Father, heal Karen's migraine in Jesus's name." And we have thanked Him for His always-good love as the headache that typically becomes a migraine fades away.

We have also prayed against a coming migraine and watched, feeling helpless, as Karen still got the migraine. And yet we are learning, even in the pain, to hurdle the disappointment that seeks to discourage our hearts, and thank Him for His always-good love.

We trusted God absolutely, financially risking everything to start a company. Karen and I watched God come through miraculously, giving us favor and increase. We thanked Him for His goodness as our company prospered.

We trusted God completely, risking everything financially by giving the company back to Him. Karen and I believed and surrendered through the debilitating season of failed business and substantial debt. We chose to thank Him for His always-good love.

We have prayed, "Lord, protect this pregnancy and our child," when a heartbeat couldn't be found. We celebrated days later in the doctor's office when life was discovered and again when our first daughter Madeleine was handed into the thankful, waiting arms of a tearfully joyful new mother and father.

We have also prayed, "Lord, protect our child and this pregnancy," when complications became obvious. And weeks later we stood in the doctor's office, grief in our eyes, as the devastating news was gently broken. On this journey of faith, we are learning, even in the midst of heartache, to trust in our Dad's always-good love.

Why? Because we have met our Dad and are convinced, and we are becoming more convinced, that our circumstances don't determine His love. He only has goodness and love for us.

"God shall supply all your needs according to His riches and glory in Christ Jesus" (Phil. 4:19 NASB). It's in my Bible and yours. That Scripture isn't a bumper sticker platitude or a warm feeling or a nice sentiment; it's a promise that His love is good. It's disappointment hurdling revelation. It's the truth. It's the truth even when we are facing sickness, bankruptcy, or death. It's the truth even when everything we are experiencing screams the lie.

The Valley

I've stood on mountains, I've knelt in valleys,
From glory to glory, my heart will always be Yours.

David was a man after God's own heart. He both started and finished well. His life was a study in mountaintops and valleys.

His story was one of miracles and misses, faith and failure. David experienced some crushing disappointments but somehow never succumbed. He ended well—better than well—he handed increase to the next generation.

I am convinced there is only one reason David succeeded where so many before and after have failed. David did not believe his circumstances were the measuring stick of God's love. On the contrary, he was convinced that God only had goodness and love for him all the days of his life. And this faith is what defined him. This faith pleased God.

"Surely goodness and love will follow me all the days of my life." It's a declaration David makes at the end of his famous Psalm 23 (verse 6). I think this line reveals how David saw God and the core conviction through which every life experience was filtered. It begins with a proclamation of God as the leader and provider of his life.

> *"The Lord is my Shepherd, I shall not be in want"* (Psalm 23:1).

David declares who God is, a Shepherd, the One he follows. He continues in the same vein.

> *"He (God) makes me lie down in green pastures, He leads me beside quiet waters, He restores my soul. He guides me in paths of righteousness for His name's sake"* (Psalm 23:2-3).

David lets us know that it is God who is leading him and that God is only leading him in good things. Then David's journey takes a desperate turn, only David isn't desperate. Notice how the language shifts in this next verse.

> *"Even though I walk through the valley of the shadow of death, I will fear no evil"* (Psalm 23:4).

I love this verse because it says something so profound about what David knew regarding God's love. "God does not lead me into the valley of the shadow of death."

While David has no problem acknowledging that valleys exist and that there are enemies in those valleys, he gives God no credit for the valley season. David's faith regarding God's always-good love for him is mind-boggling. He could follow God's goodness, experience a valley, and never blame God. Astounding!

Now here is where it gets even better. Once David finds himself in the valley, the language shifts again:

> I will fear no evil, for You are with me; Your rod and Your staff, they comfort me. You prepare a table before me in the presence of my enemies. You anoint my head with oil; my cup overflows (Psalm 23:4-5).

I love these verses! David's journey once again becomes a testament of who God is in his life. And get this: in the valley the language shifts from the early declaration of *He* to the first person intimacy of *You*. David not only knew the valley was not God's heart for him, but it was this revelation that set him free to know God in a much more intimate way.

I am convinced that David had a greater awareness of God's presence in the valley because he was never offended at God while in the valley. The valley is a place of intimate access to our heavenly Father and all His presence offers.

Somehow, David understood a New Testament revelation better than many of us now living on the other side of the cross. The revelation? God is love and He is always good. While valleys of the shadow of death exist, God does not create them—His heart for us is never death.

The last verse of Psalm 23 shows us that David truly knew the nature of God: *"Surely goodness and love will follow me all the days of my life, and I will dwell in the house of the Lord forever"* (Ps. 23:6).

David was convinced that every plan God had for him was good—*"surely goodness and love."* How else does David make it through all of his trials and still believe at the end of his life? David was able to maintain a heart after God's presence because he knew God's love was always good, that He never oscillates. Because of this, he was able to hurdle the disappointments of the valley seasons in life.

The Father Never Turned His Back, Continued

God was reconciling the world to Himself in Christ,
not counting men's sins against them.
—2 Corinthians 5:19

I saw Mel Gibson's movie *The Passion*. I was overcome by the physical abuse Jesus sustained. I grew up in church; I was taught how the horror of my sin, every sin from beginning to end, was placed on Jesus at the cross. I have been amazed by His love, that He would go through the physical torment and experience the horror of sin and death.

"For God made Christ, who never sinned, to be the offering for our sin, so that we could be made right with God through Christ" (2 Cor. 5:21 NLT). These were the realities He was facing while praying in the Garden of Gethsemane when an angel from heaven appeared to Him and strengthened Him. *"And being in anguish, He prayed more earnestly, and His sweat was like drops of blood falling to the ground"* (Luke 22:44).

While the physical pain is a part of the story and can't be overlooked, I think the greater reason He was in such anguish, the reason He sweat blood, is because He knew He was about to experience something much worse and more terrifying than physical pain. Jesus, for the first time in His life, the first and only time, would be unaware of His Father's presence.

Think about it. Jesus hadn't taken a breath without the wonder of His Dad's presence. Every thought, every experience, every heartbeat was immersed in a revelation of His Father's always-good love. Jesus lived in the lavish revelation of His Dad's presence. He lived in the sureness of His Father's love. He lived consumed by His Father's heart. That kind of intimacy is profoundly stunning.

Can you imagine an existence like that? It's my life's one ambition and it was Jesus's reality. Can you imagine your very existence being love and then having love become inaccessible and then replaced by fear, doubt, insecurity, self-loathing, hate, and every other by-product of sin?

Jesus is in a garden, and He asks His Father if the cup can be removed from Him: "Is there another way, Father?" (see Matt. 26:42). And I would like to propose, without belittling the physical sacrifice Jesus made, that the origin of Jesus's distress was in the knowledge that for the first time ever He would be separated not from His Father, but from an *awareness* of His Father.

The Son, who only did what He saw His Father doing, would not be able to see His Father. The Son, who only said what His Father said, would not be able to hear His Father. The Son, who was in the Father and in whom the Father dwelled, would not be able to know His presence, His love, His goodness. And this was a horror Jesus could hardly bear. But He did bear it, because God is love.

Jesus made Himself as a sin offering, for your sin and mine. He took sin on Himself—past, present, and future. Sin, the lie that separates us from the revelation of our Father, from an unhindered revelation of perfect love, was cloaked over Jesus like a second skin.

God hates sin; it's true.

But while Jesus became a sin offering, He never stopped being the Son. To suggest that the Father's disgust for sin somehow caused Him to abandon His Son is to suggest that just this once sin was bigger than love—and that's ridiculous.

And yet it's what I believed most of my life, that for just a moment, the Father had to excuse Himself because man's sin and Satan's power were just too much for Him to bear; for just a moment, a good Father abandoned His Son.

Jesus took on sin and in that moment He cried out, like David, *"My God, My God, why have You forsaken Me?"* And in that moment the Father stood over His Son—He hadn't left, abandoned, turned His back, or scorned His Son. He hadn't oscillated. He was there. He knew His Son couldn't *know* it, couldn't *sense* it, couldn't *feel* His always-perfect love. But He was there, loving His Boy, proud of His Son, sharing His agony, enduring the cross for the joy on the other side.

Bill Johnson and Faith

His name is Bill Johnson. He's a pastor and an author. And he's also a hero of mine. Several years ago Bill gave a message on a Sunday. He shared how it is God's heart that the measureless economy of heaven should invade the measurements of earth. He reminded us that Jesus taught us to pray, "Thy Kingdom come." He then powerfully communicated how we are called to release wholeness and health on earth as it is in heaven. He essentially said it is God's heart to heal every affliction. Always!

The week after that Sunday, Bill lost his father to cancer.

The following Sunday, Bill spoke about how it is God's desire that heaven invade earth. He reminded us that Jesus taught us to pray, "Thy Kingdom come." He then powerfully communicated how we are called to release wholeness and health on earth as it is in heaven. He essentially said it is God's heart to heal every affliction—always!

Bill has continued to live this message. And in the last years, he has seen many healed of many things, including cancer! His life has had an incredible impact on many lives, including mine.

When you hear a story like Bill Johnson's, you are moved by his faith. You say, "What a powerful testimony of enduring faith." And it is! And yet from Bill's perspective, he lost his dad to cancer.

Faith isn't just about what you believe before there's evidence; faith is also about what you believe when the evidence seems to contradict His always-good love.

"Faith is the substance of things hoped for, the evidence of things not seen" (Heb. 11:1 NKJV). Faith believes God is love and His love is always good—even under the devastating crush of disappointment, even when we can't see it.

Sometimes

Life has valleys, wildernesses, and crosses. Life is full of disappointment, disillusionment, and even death. Flesh and blood life is sometimes one overwhelming need after another. These tragedies haunt us and lie to us. These circumstances tell us that our Father isn't always good, that His love isn't perfected in His goodness.

Sometimes we find ourselves penniless, maimed, lonely, hungry, sick, feeble, lost, crushed, and under the weight of disappointment.

Sometimes our friends call to tell us they are getting divorced even though we stood with them and loved them, and cried and encouraged and saw healing and tasted hope. Sometimes there is divorce.

Sometimes the neighbor kids don't have a dad, and when they visit our hearts ache for their loneliness. Sometimes we visit an orphanage in China or Haiti or Africa and see and hear about horrors the children have faced, tragedies that make us weep with sadness.

Sometimes horrors overwhelm us, destroy us, break us. Sometimes need is so great that it's all we can see. Sometimes every breath we take is an act of faith. Sometimes we lose faith.

Sometimes Skilsaws take more than a thumb, they take everything that matters to us. Sometimes the valley of the shadow of death is the only thing that seems real. Sometimes the lie looks and sounds and feels so true.

And I am learning, that in this moment, who God is to me when I am in the valley is the most important thing ever. He is not a sometimes-God; He's an always-God.

The Father Never Turned His Back, Conclusion

This is revival, I feel it shaking the ground,
All of this glory, a deafening sound.

In the moment Jesus hung between two thieves, He couldn't see, touch, hear, or know His Dad. When Jesus became sin, He was cut off from the awareness of His Father. He had never been separated from the awareness of His Father, ever. And in the suffocating anguish of that moment, Jesus echoes a prayer from His earthly forefather David, *"My God, My God, why have You forsaken Me?"*

It's a horrible moment, a moment where hope hangs in the balance, a moment where eternity holds its breath. And in the agony of that moment the Father never turned His back, He never left, His love never soured, His goodness never faltered, His light never darkened. He never oscillated.

And then humanity is given the most powerful act of faith that has ever been. *"Jesus called out in a loud voice, 'Father, into Your hands I commit My spirit.' When He had said this, He breathed His last"* (Luke 23:46).

"Father." He called Him Father.

The greatest act of faith that was and will ever be: "I can't see You, I can't know You, I can't touch You, I can't hear You, but I believe that You are still My Father, that You will never leave or forsake Me, that

You are love, that Your love is perfect, that You only have goodness and love for Me."

"Father, into Your hands I commit My spirit."

Jesus pressed past His feelings, His circumstances, the devastating, very real sense of separation He felt, and called out to His always-good Father. Jesus believed that His Father was still there. *"Into Your hands I commit My spirit."* That's faith—pure, true, world-changing, life-saving faith.

Faith Always Leads to Resurrection

I see the night erased when the sun disappears,
I see the Kingdom come when the sun disappears.

Jesus knew the valley of the shadow of death better than anyone. The Holy Spirit led Him into the wilderness and later to the cross. And if it was the Holy Spirit who led Him and He was the Father's love perfectly revealed, then the question has to be asked: Was it the Father's heart for Jesus to starve in the wilderness? Was it the Father's heart for Jesus to die on the cross?

And by faith, the answer is no. In the wilderness it was the Father's heart to send His ministering angels. At the cross it was the Father's heart that Jesus be resurrected. It's always about the joy set before us. It's always about life—always.

And while I write this, my head is screaming at me, "That doesn't make sense." But at the same time my heart is encouraging me, whispering, "It's true." While writing this, my experiences lie to me and tell me I must be wrong about His always-good love. But faith tells another story.

Our Father's Kingdom is discovered in the unseen and is accessed through faith. This faith chooses to believe in the always-good love of our Father even when the evidence is unseen.

Is it the Father's heart that we experience pain, disillusionment, and death? Never. It's His heart that we experience peace, joy, and resurrection. His heart is always love toward us.

David experienced the valley, but the valley was never God's heart for him. Jesus went to the cross but the cross was never His focus. Death is never the focus with God. He is always and only about resurrection. Jesus faced a cross, focused on the joy of the resurrection. *"Who for the joy set before Him endured the cross"* (Heb. 12:2). What was the joy? We were His joy! Us. You and me.

Like David, I am learning to believe that the valley of the shadow of death is not my Father's heart for me. He only has goodness and love. Notice again the word *learning*.

Like Jesus, I am learning to look ahead to the sustaining joy found in the resurrection. When it comes to my Father, I am convinced that death is never the point. He is always about a future and a hope. He is always about the resurrection. He does not oscillate.

This I am learning.

Note

1. These lines are taken from the hymn "Great Is Thy Faithfulness," written by Thomas Chisholm.

Chapter Eight

THE RIGHT QUESTION

Potty Training

Years ago I had the privilege of teaching my youngest how to wipe her own bum. For those of you who don't have children and have never thought about this, you're welcome. For those of you who do, well, you know.

"First, you need four sheets," I said. I rolled off four. We counted them together. She informed me that her brother uses five.

"Well, I'll talk to him about that later," I said. "But let's start with four, okay? Watch close. We fold them in half and then again, just like this," I showed her. I continued but will spare you the rest of the details.

Just so you understand the situation, four-year-olds rarely get anything right the first few times, and they are horrible at quality control. So when you share a house with a four-year-old, there is about a fifty-fifty likelihood that the brown smudge on the bathroom light switch is either chocolate or…

Control is a nice idea in many circumstances, including potty training, but anyone who has had small children knows, control is a mirage. And it's not even the point. I don't want to control the wiping process; I want to empower the wiper.

As good parents, we spend countless hours trying to empower our children to control themselves. The goal is to someday bequeath authority down to the smallest and messiest details. Yet when it comes to our relationship with God, we tend to think He always wants more control, especially of all our smallest and messiest details.

While God is the authority on everything, and while He has the best ideas, the wisdom of the ages, and while He will gladly instruct us in even the simplest and messiest details, and while He will always be okay with brown smudges on the light switch, there is an invitation to mature, to grow, to be empowered...

Potty trained, that's what I'm trying to say.

Lazarus

All of us here, winter to spring.

You know the story. Lazarus, a good friend of Jesus, was sick. He had two devoted sisters, Mary and Martha, who sent word to Jesus. When Jesus heard about Lazarus, He said:

> *"This sickness will not end in death. No, it is for God's glory so that God's Son may be glorified through it." Jesus loved Martha and her sister and Lazarus. Yet when He heard that Lazarus was sick, He stayed where He was two more days* (John 11:4-6).

Jesus carried on, business as usual.

But just two days later, and what I imagine seemed quite out of the blue, Jesus tells His disciples it's time to go back to Judea because *"our friend Lazarus has fallen asleep; but I am going there to wake him up"* (John 11:11).

The disciples didn't understand. Jesus's actions and words didn't seem to be adding up, so He made it plain to them: *"Lazarus is dead, and for your sake I am glad I was not there, so that you may believe. But let us go to him"* (John 11:14-15).

The Right Question

The Lord always answers, but it's not as meaningful
if you don't have the questions.
—Bill Johnson

I have three kids. Eva, my youngest, was four when the questions consumed her. You know, the questions…like when I gave her a bowl of soup the other day.

"Honey, do you want some crackers for your soup?"

"Why?"

"Cause these crackers taste good in soup."

"Why?"

"Cause they are yummy soup crackers."

"Why?"

"Because the soup cracker fairy made them yummy for soup."

"What color is the soup cracker fairy's dress?"

"Blue."

"No daddy, it's pink and purple."

If you are a parent, have watched an episode of *The Cosby Show*, or have ever spoken to a child, you have laughed, sighed, had your patience stretched and your heart expanded while attempting to answer questions.

If you are a parent, have watched an episode of *The Cosby Show*, or have ever spoken to a child, you know there is such a thing as a dumb question. But you also know that if the question is sincere, then it's okay. It's how children learn. The question reveals a lot about what the child already does and doesn't comprehend and who he or she is becoming.

If you are a parent, have watched an episode of *The Cosby Show*, or have ever spoken to a child, you have often responded to a question with a question of your own.

"Mom, how do you spell dog?"

"What makes the sound *duh*?...*duh*?"

We do this because our question positions our kids for the answer. It's meant to help them learn how to process and find the answer themselves. It helps them mature.

I think our Father loves sincere questions. Jesus sure used them often enough. Have you ever noticed Jesus rarely answered a question directly? When He is asked questions, His response was often to either tell a story or ask a question of His own.

Even when Jesus did answer a question, He usually did it in a way that raised more questions. He told Nicodemus that if he wanted to enter the Kingdom of heaven, he would have to be born again. He told a large crowd, unless they ate of His flesh and drank of His blood, they had no life in them. While we now know what Jesus meant, at the time these were inconceivable thoughts that led to more questions.

Questions are one of the best ways to communicate with a free people. And Jesus was absolutely intent on releasing people into greater freedom. That's why He lived, died, and rose again.

God absolutely, and without even the slightest hint of deviation, loves our freedom. He will not compromise even a fraction when it comes to protecting it because freedom is the atmosphere in which love exists.

That's why Jesus doesn't tell free people the answer; He helps them devise a better question. So He tells stories, He asks His own questions. He makes statements like, "Lazarus is sleeping," or "I'm glad this has happened."

Along the way He challenges how we think. And if we are hungry for an answer, we begin to reform our questions until our mind is, in a word, *renewed*.

Lazarus Will Not Die

Oh, I know, how this story goes, how it all unfolds 'neath the sun.

"This sickness will not end in death…" (John 11:4).

And Jesus, only doing what the Father does and only saying what the Father says, looks to heaven and declares to everyone, including His disciples, "Lazarus will not die."

I believe this is the most important and overlooked statement in the whole Lazarus story. It's the declaration from heaven to earth upon which everything thereafter hinges. And nobody seemed to hear it. Not the fella that came and told Jesus the news of Lazarus's sickness, not His disciples, and most of us, myself included, seem to miss it.

"This sickness will not end in death…" is the most important part of the Lazarus story. Not catching that statement is like wearing a hat and gloves and nothing else—you're missing the whole point.

Missing that statement would be like watching a DVRed football game and knowing the Bills win from the beginning. It changes everything. There is no biting of the nails, no yelling at the ref, at least not with conviction, no nervous laughter, no snapping at the kids as they run in front of the TV, no guilt for snapping at the kids, no worrying over the outcome of every play.

Instead, I would watch with expectation. I'm not disappointed when an interception is thrown and I'm not disillusioned by the poor execution of the defense. I watch with hope and anticipation as each play reveals what I already know, the Bills win!

Everything that takes place after Jesus's statement is just one opportunity after another for life and love and the goodness of our Father to be experienced, embraced, and believed.

Jesus told everyone the end of the story.

But as the story unfolds, it becomes very apparent no one heard Him. And to this day there are still many who have missed it. It's easy to do if we think God wants control, if we aren't becoming sure in the authority of our Father's love.

Good Aim

A parent's journal:

> My son went pee pee on the potty today—all by himself! When I was single it never crossed my mind that someday this would be cause for celebration. If someone told me in my future the highlight of a day would be cheering a two-year-old because of a successful trip to the bathroom, I would have thought that person daft.

I don't know how many times I have encouraged with such passion: "Aim down, aim down! You did it! Yay!"

The day my boy walked in the authority to control himself was a day of celebration—all heaven joined in the party!

But isn't that what a good father wants, to give authority and empower sons and daughters so they can mature and control themselves?

What if love has nothing to do with control and everything to do with authority and power?

What Would Have Happened?

Lazarus lived in Bethany, which was near Jerusalem. This was a big deal. In fact, it was the circumstance by which the disciples filtered everything regarding Lazarus. When Jesus first declared Lazarus's future, the only thing the disciples heard was, "We don't have to go back to Jerusalem." And the only thought they had was, "Oh, thank God." You see, they had just been violently escorted out of Jerusalem under the threat of stoning.

Stoning is a brutal way to die. Your body is cut and pierced, your bones are broken; you are essentially beaten to a pulp until dead. If it has almost happened, I imagine it kinda leaves an impression.

I believe the disciples near-death experience loomed larger in their memory than the miraculous healings they'd seen up to this point. Their fear hindered them from recognizing that Jesus had answered the question.

Lazarus was deathly ill, that was the "question." *"This sickness will not end in death"* was the answer.

Have you ever wondered what would have happened if the fella who came from Jerusalem to report Lazarus's sickness had truly heard Jesus answer the question and immediately headed back to tell Mary and Martha the good news? Lazarus may have never had to be entombed. Seriously. Jesus had already performed the miracle.

Only a short time before, a centurion sent friends to ask Jesus to simply declare his servant's healing. Essentially, he told Jesus, "I understand authority. You don't need to come to my house, just say it and my servant will be healed" (see Luke 7:6-8).

> *When Jesus heard this, He was amazed at him* (the centurion), *and turning to the crowd following Him, He said, "I tell you, I have not found such great faith even in Israel." Then the men who had been sent returned to the house and found the servant well* (Luke 7:9-10).

If the fella bringing the news of Lazarus's sickness had centurion-like faith in what Jesus declared, he could have run home with the good news!

What if the disciples had truly heard Jesus? Maybe one of them could have had faith for Lazarus? They were there when Jesus was mesmerized, amazed, astounded, and pleased by the radical, breathtaking, powerful faith of the centurion.

When Jesus heard this, He was astonished and said to those following Him, "I tell you the truth, I have not found anyone in Israel with such great faith" (Matthew 8:10).

What if one of the disciples would have remembered this great centurion's faith during the whole Lazarus incident?

When Jesus said, "Lazarus will not die," it was kinda like the parent prompting the child, "What makes the sound *duh?...duh?*" This was an opportunity for the disciples to mature, to ask the right question; the right question that would give them access to the miraculous answer.

It's amazing how we can witness God move miraculously in our lives, and yet the next time we are in a similar situation, we forget what He did for us. Our historical amnesia kicks in so quickly.

Lazarus Is Sleeping

I know what you're hiding from,
And I know where we're going too...

In my hands is an average top hat. "Yes, you! Come up on stage, young lady. Give her a hand, ladies and gentlemen."

A young girl walks timidly onto the stage. She's shy. Clearly she has never stood in front of people before; she's terribly uncomfortable. We can all feel it, it adds to the show.

"Young lady, if you would be so kind as to stick your hand inside the hat. Go ahead, it won't bite."

The magician smiles at the audience as if he might be lying. He's quite the showman.

"Yes, inspect it thoroughly. That's good!" he purrs. "Now, would you say this is a normal top hat? Nothing special, no tricks, no...rabbits?" He grins, both giving everyone a clue of what's to come and fueling expectation.

She nods, smiling in agreement. She's convinced and so are all of us. But we are hoping, even expecting to be proved wrong.

And then the magician does something spectacular; he reaches his hand into the top hat and pulls out a rabbit!

He was looking to dazzle, and he does! We are in awe!

"How did he do it?" a wide-eyed boy asks his mom.

"It's magic," she says.

And for a moment we believe.

A good magician can suspend reality; a really good magician can make us believe. He waves and shouts, smiles and winks, and along the way he convinces us time and space can be manipulated. He inspires faith in the possibility of an invisible realm and makes us believe the impossible just might be possible.

"Lazarus is sleeping." This is what Jesus says about Lazarus after he has died.

Jesus wouldn't have made a good magician. Don't get me wrong. His ability to inspire awe and increase faith, to make you believe in the impossible becoming possible, was unparalleled. But regarding setup, timing, and His interest in self-branding, He was lacking.

Think about it. He was always doing miracles, then commanding the recipients of the miracle not to tell anyone. He almost slept through the calming of the storm. When He walked on water, He did it at night after the crowds had dispersed. And then, when He is about to raise the dead, His greatest awe-inspiring miracle of all, the "showstopper" if you will, He refers to the dead person as "sleeping."

At least three times Jesus raises the dead as recorded in the Gospels. One time He was walking through a city called Nain and happened across a funeral procession. He completely ruined the funeral. Moved with compassion, He walked up to the open coffin, and told the young man to "rise." And the young man arose (see Luke 7:11-17).

Then there was Jarius's daughter in Matthew 9:23-25 (NKJV):

When Jesus came into the ruler's house, and saw the flute players and the noisy crowd wailing, He said to them, "Make room, for the girl is not dead, but sleeping." And they ridiculed Him. But when the crowd was put outside, He went in and took her by the hand, and the girl arose.

And finally there is the story of Lazarus.

"Lazarus is sleeping." It's the same word He used with Jarius's daughter.

It's an odd statement. *"Lazarus is sleeping,"* is a rather anticlimactic way to explain the situation.

If Jesus really wanted to thrill His audience, if He really wanted to capitalize on this tragedy, if He really wanted to use pain and sadness to grow faith, to convince His followers, His audience, that He was God's Son, that His Father was powerful and in control, if Jesus was a good magician, He wouldn't have referred to a dead person as sleeping.

People's minds aren't blown when a sleeper is awakened. I do it every morning with no fanfare. None of my kids are impressed by my faith when I rouse them from slumber. I think waking someone up is a substandard miracle at best. No self-respecting magician would perform such a flimsy excuse for a trick. But Jesus wasn't a good magician.

Can you picture Jesus after He said Lazarus was sleeping? I bet He paused a moment. I imagine a smile graced the corners of His mouth while a look of hope hinted in His eyes. He waited for one of His disciples to remember the last time He had referred to a dead person as sleeping. But Jesus wasn't a good magician; He was too subtle and no one caught His clue. His disciples only had one memory and it wasn't about resurrection life—just the opposite.

But what if they hadn't been so anxiously distracted by the thought of what potentially waited for them back in Jerusalem? What if they had heard Jesus use the same phrase He had used at least once before?

What makes the sound *duh?...duh?* Jesus was prompting again, giving the disciples an opportunity to ask the right question.

Jesus waited a few more seconds, the moment pregnant with possibilities. And then, realizing the boys hadn't truly heard Him as He described Lazarus from heaven's perspective, Jesus describes Lazarus in the language of earth, *"Lazarus is dead"* (John 11:14). But before anyone could blink, He shifted right back to the language of heaven: *"This is good, because it's another opportunity for you to grow in faith"* (John 11:15 paraphrase).

Then Thomas, one of Jesus's disciples, makes a statement that best captures the losing wrestling match taking place in the hearts of the disciples: "Well, I guess we will go back to Jerusalem and die with Him" (John 11:16 paraphrase).

Die with whom? Jesus? Lazarus? It really didn't matter; death was death, or was it?

Childlike Faith = Heaven's Perspective

"And He said: 'I tell you the truth, unless you change and become like little children, you will never enter the kingdom of heaven'" (Matt. 18:3).

Childlike wonder is how we access the measureless revelation of heaven. Our faith is directly connected with our childlikeness. Children will ask the wrong question until they ask the right one—the question that releases the answer. Unless we become like a child, we can't truly hear, experience, or access our Father. Thankfully, everyone I know of has been a child at least once in their life.

But it's hard to stay childlike when there is disappointment, pain, fear, and death; when the needs of life seek to control.

Need gets louder and more forceful as we grow from a child to an adult. Need becomes more belligerent and ugly the older we get; it becomes more violent and oppressive as we mature.

Need will demand from us our faith.

Need will try and strip from us our childlike wonder. It will try to separate us from the measureless revelation of love. It will endeavor to cut us off from dreaming. Need will lead us into disappointment and sorrow and pain and heartache and loneliness, and there is nothing we can do about it, except choose to stay childlike as we mature in the authority of love.

When we were children, God could cleanse the leper, heal the sick, cast out darkness, and wake the dead. That's the power Love has, that's the authority Love gives.

"Lazarus is sleeping," is the way a child would have described the situation as well.

From earth's perspective, Lazarus was dead. From heaven's perspective, death looked like an afternoon nap.

Jesus Wept

And I know it won't be easy, oh honey, I know,
Wait and see and please be patient,
all creation's groaning for its home.
—Scott Crowder[1]

When Jesus arrived in Bethany, Lazarus was four days dead. Martha met Him on the edge of town. She was disappointed and let Him know: *"If You had been here, my brother would not have died"* (John 11:21). And then:

"Jesus wept" (John 11:35).

Isn't that stunning?

Even though Jesus knew Lazarus was just sleeping, even though He knew Lazarus would be raised in moments, even though He knew the end of the story, He still wept with Mary and Martha.

I love Jesus for this! He always honors us while at no time manipulating our pain. He so values our hearts that He positions Himself in our pain. There is something profoundly beautiful in this expression of love. But it shouldn't surprise us as Jesus only does what He sees the Father doing. And, of course, the Father was weeping; it's what a good Father would do.

When my two-year-old baby girl begins to cry because Mom has just gone out the front door to get the mail, I scoop her up and tell her that it's going to be okay. I love on her, I hold her, I whisper in her ear, "I got you, honey." Even though I know her mom will be right back, I don't devalue what she is feeling. She doesn't yet have the ability to understand that Mom is just on the other side of the door. Her distress is real. What kind of dad would I be if I couldn't value her journey?

Jesus weeps with those who weep. He doesn't celebrate their pain so that later, when their pain has turned into joy, they will know that He is a good God—that makes no sense. But how many of us serve that kind of a nonsense God?

I believe there was a second reason Jesus wept. He wept for the state and condition of humanity. I think He wept because He was in the midst of a fallen world, a faithless world, a world controlled by death, a world that couldn't be sure in the power and authority of His love; a world where He had healed the sick and raised the dead and still no one, including His disciples and closest friends, believed. He witnessed the ravaging sickness that Adam's sin positioned humanity in, and He wept.

His heart broke because there was no faith for resurrection life.

And then Jesus calls Lazarus forth.

And Lazarus wakes up! Revived, revival! And sorrow is turned into laughter.

Control

The thief comes only to steal and kill and destroy; I have
come that they may have life, and have it to the full.
—John 10:10

I believe much of the church has often represented a God who is about control instead of authority, manipulation instead of freedom, shame instead of love.

God never instigates nor manipulates a tragedy to grow faith—that's not what a good Father does. But it is what a controlling God would do. To suggest God assists in evil things happening to us for our own good is to suggest that God partners with the enemy to grow our faith. It's ridiculous. He is either always good or He is bipolar.

I wonder if part of the reason we have such a rash of bipolar in the Western world is because much of the church teaches a God who is *almost* always good. You just never know what you are gonna get with Him, He is high one day and low the next.

I would like to suggest that many of us live a "mostly good gospel" because we know a "mostly good God."

When we read the Lazarus story through the lens of a controlling God, then we have to put the death of Lazarus at the feet of Jesus. Worse, we have to assume Jesus partnered with death, the result of sin, to bring life. The lie that God wants to control us forces us to manipulate pain and death into a perversion of love.

To suggest that Jesus partners with sin and death to reveal His always-good love is intellectually, and in every other way, dishonest. The idea that God is good and the idea that God wants control are two opposing thoughts. And yet I have heard this God taught my whole life.

As if He is a good God who wants control of our lives and will part-ner with evil to get it; a good God who will compromise our freedom by manipulating evil circumstances to gain our affections; a good God who will allow love to be distorted and perverted to capitalize on our needs; a good God who is an accessory to murder, starvation, sickness, and poverty so that we could know how much He loves us. The contradiction between control and His goodness is of epic proportions. It can't be further from the truth. God is not about control!

But He does have all authority.

Authority and Power

All of our seasons, all of our dreams,
All of our stories, the wonder of kings.

Jesus didn't reveal a controlling God; He revealed the authority and power of our Father's always-good love.

Authority and power is the perfection of His love. It operates from the measureless revelation of love. It looks like Jesus. It heals blind eyes, it cleanses lepers, it feeds the hungry, it clothes the poor, it raises the dead, it loves, it loves, it loves!

And it sets free and it redeems and it restores and it transforms sinners to saints and slaves to sons. And it looks like heaven. Here. Now. It has hands and feet, you and me, and we look like Jesus!

And it's measureless; it knows no end, no boundaries, no lack. And it trumps every controlling need. That's the authority and power of love—as opposite to control as darkness is to light.

Control < Authority

Your heart be our compass, to be known by Your love,
And we'll cling to Your promise, You're waking the dead.

"And we know that in all things God works for the good of those who love Him…" (Rom. 8:28).

Be careful, for that's not a description of what He does. It's a description of the power and authority of His love. The Scripture doesn't suggest God endorses bad things happening to us so we can have more faith. It says He redeems even bad things for our good. He is the relentless Redeemer, the One who restores. He is good and therefore He can't help but work things to good for those that say yes to His love.

The fact that the disciples grew in faith through Lazarus's death and resurrection was the evidence of His goodness, not the evidence of a God with a bipolar nature. The faith the disciples were wrestling with had nothing to do with Lazarus and everything to do with them facing the fears of a murderous, stone-happy, Jerusalem mob.

The disciples didn't understand. All they could see was the impending possibility of a horrific death. But this story was never about death. Remember, Lazarus wasn't going to die. When Jesus said, *"I'm glad I was not there, so that you may believe,"* He wasn't saying He was glad Lazarus died—that was never the destination—but He was glad Lazarus would be raised. Jesus revealed to His disciples and all of us that it's never about death; it's always about resurrection life. Please get this: my story and your story are never about death, they are always about resurrection life.

I absolutely believe God is sovereign, but I won't use the word *control* to describe it. I am convinced God's sovereignty is discovered, founded, and originates in His always-good love and it looks like authority and power.

I'll communicate the authority and power of His love with every breath as I have discovered a great transforming freedom and empowering faith in this revelation. I have discovered that control is always about measurements, but authority is always about the measureless; control will destroy faith but power will birth revival.

Jesus said, *"All authority in heaven and on earth has been given to Me. Therefore go and make disciples..."* (Matt. 28:18-19). Essentially

He was saying, "I have all of the authority and now I'm giving it to you. Now go wake up the sleepers."

Authority is the maturity of love; it's powerful and it wakes the sleeper up.

Conclusion

I started this chapter off by suggesting that God is patiently and eagerly seeking to empower us that we might come into maturity, to walk in the authority of His love—potty trained is the amusing vernacular I used. God doesn't want to control us; His greatest desire is to give us authority.

The story of Lazarus is filled with plenty of opportunities for the disciples to mature in their childlike faith, to live from the measureless revelation of heaven, to ask the questions Jesus was prompting, the questions that would release revelation and faith. But when you live in the context of control, you are enslaved to the inferior demanding reality of need.

Jesus has given us the end of our story. We win! He said *all* authority has been given to Him, and then He commissioned us, giving us the same authority (see Matt. 28:18). He is daily prompting us, "What makes the sound *duh?...duh?*" He is daily inviting us to discover the authority and power of love.

> *God, give us childlike hearts that ask the right questions,*
> *ears to hear, and eyes to see the revelation of Love that raises*
> *the dead.*

Note

1. These lyrics are taken from Scott Crowder's album *Upon Shoulders*, http://scottcrowder.bandcamp.com/album/upon-shoulders.

Chapter Nine

PRONE TO LOVE

Grandma Eva

Let Your love be all I know,
Till Your glory becomes my own.

Grandma's lips always moved. If you were close enough, you could sometimes catch a few phrases.

"Thank You, Jesus. I love You, Jesus. You are so precious."

Elmer and Eva were the kindest and most gracious people on the planet. I am not exaggerating. They never spoke harshly of anyone; they were never critical and always generous. What they had was yours.

My dad tells stories from his childhood about how the neighbor boys referred to Grandma as the "God lady." They would sneak into the Clark house anytime of the day and help themselves to the cookies in the cookie jar. Apparently, one day Grandma caught them red-handed. Then she kindly said, "Now boys, you can have cookies whenever you want. You don't need to sneak, all you need to do is ask."

There is a verse in Daniel that describes my grandparents: *"But the saints of the Most High will receive the kingdom and possess it forever—yes, for ever and ever"* (Dan. 7:18). My grandma and grandpa, they were those saints. When you were around them, you could almost taste it, smell it, feel it—heaven was that close.

My grandparents lived in God's love. They gave over half their income to missions and their home was open to everyone. A holy hostel of sorts, a safe place for the wanderer, the hurting, and the hungry. There was almost always someone living with them. In my twenties, I often wondered if some of these people took advantage of their generosity. But looking back, I realize now that it's impossible to take advantage of love.

Grandpa lived to be ninety-five; he went home first. Grandma followed at the age of one hundred. After Grandma died, I miraculously found myself in possession of an amazing, holy, historical, Clark inheritance—her Bible. I remember helping pack up some of my grandparents' things at their house. Somehow, I ended up with the box containing Grandpa's cool Sinatra hat and Grandma's Bible.

It honestly wasn't intentional. But when I realized I had Grandma's Bible, and that no one in my family knew it, well, let's just say I was tempted beyond what I could almost bear. I'm not proud of this, but it took me weeks to let the cat out of the bag. Personally, I thought it was God's will. My family thought otherwise.

Dad finally sequestered it, but not before I had a chance to read through and scan some of the contents. That said, I still have Grandpa's Sinatra body and soul fedora hat and it's the way he wanted it, so leave off!

I realize I am going on about this Bible, but you have to understand this was hers for over fifty years! Some of my heritage as a child of the King has been documented and preserved in its pages. It was like having a personalized road map to my inheritance. This Bible is marked on nearly every page and in every color of ink you can imagine. It is filled with intimate notes in the margins about God's grace and mercy and kindness, but most of all, His love.

In fact, God's love seemed to be the singular pursuit of my grandmother. There were several handwritten notes and poems she had cut out of papers and magazines:

> For the love of God is broader than the measure of man's mind.
>
> And the heart of the Eternal is most wonderfully kind.[1]

And,

> He drew a circle that shut me out,
>
> Heretic, rebel, a thing to flout.
>
> But Love and I had the wit to win,
>
> We drew a circle that took him in![2]

Honestly, while writing this, I am overwhelmed and infinitely grateful by how my grandparents lived. They truly were world changers, heroes in the faith, saints. They lived in such an intimate friendship with Jesus and their prayers never ceased for their kids, their grandkids, and their great-grandkids.

Even though they are now in heaven, I still feel the echoes of their prayers. I see the evidence in my life and in the lives of my kids. I am their legacy, as are my kids, and so on. And that's the way it's supposed to be. You see, when saints pray, the Kingdom is possessed, today and for the ages that come.

My cousins, Chris and Jonathan, had the privilege of growing up in the same town as my grandparents. Since my grandparents passed away, I have heard many stories about their lives. Recently, however, I heard a new story about Grandma Eva as told by my cousin Jonathan that absolutely amazed me. I recognized it immediately because it is my story as well; it was a mile marker on my journey into my Father's always-good love. But it's not just for me. I believe I am meant to share it with you as well.

Grandma and Grandpa went to their church whenever there was a service. They participated in every way. Jonathan was with Grandma one Sunday morning. During worship, he noticed she was not singing the words. See, Grandma was a worshiper; she always sang.

The congregation was well into the famous and beautiful hymn "Come Thou Fount." As Jonathan tells it, Grandma was not only *not* singing, she seemed uncharacteristically agitated.

The piano led the voices:

> *And let Thy goodness, like a fetter,*
> *Bind my wandering heart to Thee.*

To Jonathan, Grandma's lack of participation bordered on stubbornness.

> *Prone to wander, Lord, I feel it,*
> *Prone to leave the God I love.*

Grandma seemed perturbed by this line. She was the most patient and kind woman on the planet. Perturbed was so out of character for her that Jonathan became concerned. Finally, he leaned over.

"Grandma, what's wrong?" he whispered.

Grandma said, "I'm not prone to wander, Jonathan. I love Him!"

Adam and Eve—Minty Fresh

> *Righteous as the first dawn...*
> —Band of a Thousand[3]

I married an angel. She still is. Her smile consumes my heart, her intellect is stunning, her fierce love for our kids and me is better than even the wildest imaginings I had before we married.

And yes, before we married I had wild imaginings. And while many and more have been surpassed, others have foundered in the sober light of reality.

First, I have discovered that nighttime is primarily for sleeping. Second, my soda is still her soda, and it's no longer as cute. Third, I now sit down when I pee; it's just easier that way.

But these realities pale in comparison to the disappointing tragedy that is the morning kiss. Hollywood has lied to us! Their portrayal of the morning kiss is heartbreaking in its audacious deceit.

You've seen the movie.

The fella wakes up in the morning, the sun is shining through the bedroom window. He rolls over; his beauty is sleeping next to him. She is radiant. "Good morning, gorgeous," he says. Her eyes are closed but she smiles. Then she stretches, opens her glorious eyes, and rolls into his arms. And they kiss. And it's not a light peck; it's a full-on, let's-include-the-tongue kiss.

And it's a outright lie! Morning breath is real, it's ugly, and it's the silent killer.

But there was once a better time, long ago…

Eve was lying in a pile of fig leaves next to Adam; he had just woken up and was stretching. The sun was shining; she could feel it on her skin. She kept her eyes closed and waited. She felt the leafy bed move as he rolled toward her. She pretended to sleep, knowing her perfection was being adored. "Good morning, gorgeous," he said. She couldn't help it, she smiled, and then stretching, she opened her glorious eyes, and rolled into his embrace. And they kissed.

It was a passionate kiss, a celebration of love. But more than that, it was a celebration of perfection—their minty fresh morning breath a tribute to the wonder that was their existence. In case you were wondering, before sin, morning breath was minty fresh.

Yes, much was lost in the fall.

You see, Adam and Eve were perfect—made in the image and likeness of Perfection.

"Come Thou Fount"

Robert Robinson was born in 1735. He lost his father at the age of ten. His mother, believed to have been a strong Christian, had a desire to see her son grow up to become a minister. However, Robert was willfully lost. When he turned fourteen, his mother sent him to London to apprentice with a barber. For the next several years Robert lived a life of drinking and gambling. He was prone to wander.

At the age of seventeen, he and his drinking buddies went to a meeting where revivalist George Whitfield was preaching. Apparently they were planning on mocking those in attendance. But upon hearing the message, Robert's heart was assaulted by Love.

For the following three years Robert wrestled with God. In 1755, at the age of twenty, he won by surrendering. As a side note, God won too. It's what we in the Kingdom call a win/win!

Three years after Robert said yes to Love, he composed a song. This song is amazing in its revelation.

Come, Thou Fount of every blessing,
Tune my heart to sing Thy grace;
Streams of mercy, never ceasing,
call for songs of loudest praise.
Teach me some melodious sonnet,
sung by flaming tongues above.
Praise the mount! I'm fixed upon it,
Mount of Thy redeeming love.

The song has four stanzas in total and for the last 250 years it has captured hearts with the authority of its revelation. The lyrics and melody coalesce beautifully to reveal and release the wonder of grace and the power of love. Many have sung it while in their own wrestling match with God. There have been many win/win's because of Robert's revelation.

This song was Robert's story. It was a testimony of one sinner's journey to the "mount of Thy redeeming love!" It's the prodigal son epic. It's one of the most enduring stories in the universe because it's not just Robert's, it's ours. Every one of us who have said yes to Love have tasted and touched, been immersed and redeemed, restored and made whole.

All of us are on a journey like Robert's. We live to discover our Father's love. And while this song is powerful in that revelation, the journey doesn't end at the discovery. It's just the beginning.

Adam and Eve—Two Trees

Eve thought about the kiss and giggled. It had been a sweet morning. That kiss had led to beautiful conversation and other things that are really none of our business. Later, over breakfast, they planned their day.

Adam told her he was going to name another animal after her. It was a small, quick, sleek four-legged creature. He would call it foxy. The name has since been abbreviated.

Eve told Adam about how she wanted to go pick some wild spinach as she had a great idea for a salad that evening. That's what she was up to when she walked past the tree and met the snake.

There were two trees in the Garden. Well, there were probably thousands of trees in the Garden, but there were two particular trees God went out of His way to acknowledge.

First, the tree of life. It was the good tree, the one that represents the fulfillment of our deepest longing, the measureless revelation of heaven as Psalm 13:2 states.

Then there was the tree of the knowledge of good and evil. That was the one with the bad apples. God gave some simple instructions about these two trees: "Help yourself to the tree of life, but stay away from them bad apples."

The reason for two trees? It was about love, it was about freedom. Love is always about our freedom. He will not compromise even a fraction when it comes to protecting it. In Galatians 5:1, Paul made a rather obvious statement about this: *"It is for freedom that Christ has set us free."* Jesus died and rose for our freedom. And through Him we are set free to choose—love or need?

Freedom, it's about choice. It's the atmosphere in which love can exist. It's the soil in which love can grow. The fact is, if you can't choose to *not* love, you can't choose *to* love.

That's why He gave Adam and Eve two trees—a choice, love or need?

I don't think Adam and Eve truly knew what need was while living in the Garden. At least not the overwhelming heartache, crisis of identity, insecurity need that all of us face. In fact, they were so clueless about need that they walked around naked.

So while I don't know what their morning pillow talk entailed, I'd imagine their conversations were more focused on all the dreams and potential a perfect God, a perfect son and daughter, and a perfect relationship with Love would have to offer.

Can you imagine it? No insecurity, no overwhelming need, no sickness, hopelessness, heartache; just the Father's love perfectly encountered, embraced, revealed, and experienced in every relationship you know, every interaction, every thought.

My guess is that Adam and Eve dreamed together and their dreams were always good, they dreamed the very heart of God. They dreamed of all the things they could do in a world designed for just the two of them. And their dreams didn't include need or lack as they didn't know need or lack, they only knew love.

These two people were made in the image of God. Without spot or blemish. Adam and Eve were in perfect alignment with God. Their relationship did not even have a hint of a lie in it. It was pure and beautiful.

It was whole, absolutely transparent. It was flawless in mind, heart, and soul. Because they were made in God's image, they were sinless. They were like God— perfect.

Perfect, that's the word.

And that's why I think they probably felt the same way about God as my grandma did that day at church. They weren't prone to wonder, they loved Him.

I believe that when your mind is pure and your heart is full of love, sinning isn't something you want to do. It's not even really that tempting.

My point is that I don't think the bad fruit was enticing. I doubt they spent much time, if any at all, thinking or talking about the bad apples. I honestly don't believe it was even on their radar. I'm not saying that they weren't capable of thinking about it; I simply don't believe they did. Neither do I believe that it was a part of their daily conversations.

When Maddy was two and a half, she discovered the TV ON button, which was tragically, and not for long, within her reach. One afternoon when we had company, and after she had turned the TV on twenty-five times, and after Karen or I had turned it off twenty-five times, we decided to try our hand at parenting. "No touch, honey," we said, and we meant it.

Now Maddy wasn't happy about this and she let us know. For the next ten minutes she would wobble up to the TV, point at the ON button, and say, "No, no, no." Then she'd take a stroll through the family room, crying as if her little heart couldn't bear the immense sorrow of not being able to push the button. Before long she was back in front of the TV letting us know her pain. Finally, when she couldn't take it anymore, and as we sat dumbfound and bemused, she looked at us and wailed, "No, no, no, no," as she reached her hand out and touched it.

I think everyone who has taken a breath has felt this—the desire to do something you've been told you shouldn't. And because we can all relate, it's easy to project that same desire on Adam and Eve. Our theology is too often constructed to support our personal experiences instead of being determined by the Word of God—perfect Love. The tree of knowledge was not like the TV button, this all-consuming thought, an agonizing battle. And yet many of us view it that way. But there is no evidence in the Bible to support it.

Adam wasn't plagued with thoughts of bad apples. He didn't walk around trying to be good while battling the urge to defy God.

"Name the animals; don't eat the apples. Go for a walk with Eve; don't eat the apples. Build a tree fort; don't eat the apples. Make orange juice; don't eat the apples…"

I would like to suggest that neither Adam nor Eve spent their days battling with sinful thoughts. Never. Perfect people who are made so because of God's perfect love don't naturally want to sin.

Adam and Eve didn't spend their days trying not to sin. Nor were they intrigued by it. I don't think they ever desired to eat the bad apple. Their DNA was holy, just like their Dad's. Humanity was originally designed and created in His image, prone to love.

So here's a question, and it's a big one: Whose idea was it to disobey God? Eve's? Adam's?

Here is my crazy thought: original sin didn't originate in the mind of man.

I am not saying Adam and Eve didn't have the capacity to think of defying God. But the fact is, that's just not how it happened. And it makes sense. Adam and Eve shared the same DNA as Father God. They were secure and whole in His love.

The Conversation

I'm becoming like You…

I ran into a fellow believer the other day at Starbucks. I was leaving and she was just arriving. It didn't take long, however, before we both found a seat as our conversation was invaded by God's always-good love.

After quick hellos, our discussion stumbled into a topic much debated at church water coolers across the U.S. She wanted to know my thoughts regarding a controversial Christian book that had recently been released. I hadn't read the book at the time, so I had no opinion on its content. But I sure loved the title. I told her so.

Then, almost as an aside, she asked, "Are you writing anything controversial these days?"

"Not in my opinion," I laughed. "That said, I have discovered that many Christians find one of my messages to be controversial." Having missed out on the first controversy, she was game for a new one. "What is it?" she asked, smiling.

"Did you know that both you and I are prone to love Him, we are righteous, we are inherently good; when we said yes to God our actual DNA became holy?"

I watched her face as I spoke. By the time I was finished telling her how amazing we were, I could tell that we had found something "controversial" to talk about. I was excited because it's always fun to tell someone how our Father sees them.

I laughed, "You don't believe me, do you?"

She smiled, "Well, I guess…I have always been taught that we have a sinful nature. What do you mean by prone to love Him?"

That's when I told her about my grandmother. Then, because she didn't know my grandmother, I threw a few Scriptures in to make it legal.

> In the same way, count yourselves dead to sin but alive to God in Christ Jesus (Romans 6:11).

And,

> For you died, and your life is now hidden with Christ in God (Colossians 3:3).

And,

If anyone is in Christ, he is a new creature: old things passed away; behold, new things have come (2 Corinthians 5:17 NASB).

And,

Put on the new self, created to be like God in true righteousness and holiness (Ephesians 4:24).

And,

No one who is born of God will continue to sin, because God's seed remains in them; they cannot go on sinning, because they have been born of God (1 John 3:9).

I continued, "When we said yes to Jesus, our old sinful nature died with Him on the cross. The old self, or the 'old things' passed away; they're dead. We are now new creations in Christ; we are created to be like God in true righteousness and holiness."

Over the next half hour I shared about how our heavenly Father always looks at us through the lens of Jesus's death and resurrection, and therefore He always likes what He sees. Not only does He look at us through His Son, but He has invited us to agree with Him regarding how He sees us.

While we may often feel like spiritual dwarfs, He sees us as spiritual giants. While we may occasionally act like sinners, He still treats us like saints. While we may be convinced we are prone to wander, He believes we are prone to love. The journey all believers are on is a journey like that of my grandmother. We live to discover our Father's love and become transformed until one day we can agree with God not just about His nature, but also about our own.

I could see as I talked that she was becoming both excited and also a little nervous. She was excited because just maybe it was true, and, if so, it was wonderfully good news. She was nervous because, well, she has lived a long time with herself.

You Look Even Better than You Feel

This love, this revival, it's shaking the ground,
All of this glory, a deafening sound.

Ethan recently got a brand new Buffalo Bills jersey. When he walked into the room wearing it, he was smiling ear to ear. Then he asked me an awesome question: "Dad, do I look as good as I feel?"

I laughed, "Son, you look even better than you feel!"

I think the reason it is so easy to believe we are prone to wander is because we have all done some wandering. We have all turned our backs on Love; we have all sinned. I get it. I have lived with me my whole life. I have had a front row seat to my failures. I've been there when I did something that I am not proud of.

That said, this whole "prone to love Him" thing is about faith. Faith is not discovered in our feelings, it's not determined by our surroundings, and it's not controlled by our past. Faith is birthed in the discovery of our Father's nature. And it's always about a future and a hope. In fact, *"Faith is the substance of things hoped for, the evidence of things not seen"* (Heb. 11:1 NKJV). While it takes no faith to believe we are prone to wander, it takes great faith to believe we are prone to love Him.

Paul told us that without faith, we couldn't please God (see Heb. 11:6). It's a leap of amazing faith to agree with our Father regarding our righteous nature when there is plenty of evidence to prove otherwise. And I'm convinced this is the "faith" that truly pleases Him.

You see, faith is the currency of our Father's Kingdom, and what we spend our faith on determines how we live. If I believe I am evil, then every bad thought confirms it. If I believe I am unholy, then every failure confirms it. If I believe I am unworthy, then instead of running to my Father's always-good love in the midst of temptation or hardship, I hide. If I believe I am prone to wander simply because I have in the past, then I've determined that my past is more powerful than my Father's love. If I believe I am prone to leave God because I feel like it, then my feelings might as well be my gospel.

My hero, Kris Vallotton, says it this way: "If you believe you are a sinner, then by faith you will sin." And the opposite is also true: if you believe you are a saint, then by faith you will live righteous.

I am on an amazing journey in which I am discovering the same thing my grandmother discovered. Because of Jesus's life, death, and resurrection, and because I have said yes to Him, I am no longer prone to wander. Just the opposite, I am prone to love Him! The moment I said yes to Jesus, my very nature underwent a radical transformation.

I am growing in my Father's love. I am growing in faith. I am choosing to believe that what Jesus did on the cross was enough and in Him, well, I look good! I am choosing to see myself from my Father's perspective and agree with Him. And every time I see myself through Dad's eyes, I hear Him say, "Son, you look even better than you feel!"

Dear church, I would like to suggest that we are holy by nature. Our DNA changed the moment we said yes to Jesus, and we are now righteous. We are saints. Our heavenly Father sees us through the love of His Son. He sees the goodness in our hearts. He sees the love that we have for others. He sees world-changing generosity, mercy, grace, and kindness. He sees spiritual giants who will transform the world with His love. If we would just take the leap of faith and agree with Him, oh, the things we would see!

Adam and Eve—Original Value

There was a snake. He could talk. He made a suggestion. It was a lie. Eve believed the lie.

The lie? We've covered this already—God is about control and He is keeping something from you. His love isn't perfect. He isn't always good. He is not enough. He is withholding, uncaring, disinterested. An egomaniac, a liar, blah, blah, blah.

When we lose track of God's nature, we become deceived about our own. That's what happens when a lie is believed; it separates us from His love nature and our identity as sons and daughters.

And that's just what happened to Eve and then to Adam. They made a choice to believe a lie regarding God's always-good love.

Whenever we discuss this great tragedy, we tend to focus on the choice, the sinful decision. But what I want to focus on is who supplied the lie.

The thought to disobey God didn't originate with Eve. It was the serpent's idea, he whispered into Eve's ear. And neither was it Adam's idea when he joined her in rebellion. Eve simply passed the lie along.

Understand me. I am not absolving Adam and Eve. They made a choice to walk away from a perfect love relationship; they chose to give their God-given authority and freedom to Satan. It was a big deal. I am simply pointing out that the idea to sin didn't originate with them, which I also think is a big deal. Why? Well, I think it says a lot about our original value, how God designed and created us.

You see, most of my life I have been told that I had a proclivity to sin, that it was actually a part of my DNA. However, in the last several years I have come to understand that the moment I said yes to Love I was redeemed and restored to my original value. My original value is not a sinner.

Sin didn't first enter the world through the hearts or minds of a man. It came from a lie provided by Satan. It wasn't Adam or Eve's nature to sin that led them to sin. It was a lie believed that distorted the perfect love nature of their heavenly Father. This is groundbreaking revelation. Why? Because many Christians walk around this planet beating themselves over the head battling a nature that through Christ's death and resurrection doesn't even exist.

We are no longer sinners!

When the options for me to choose to live righteous or sinful start with a lie about my nature being sinful, I'm caught between survival and insecurity.

Most of my life I didn't know I am not a sinner, that I am no longer prone to wander. I had been taught a lie. And sadly, it's been primarily Christians doing the teaching.

A Headlong Discovery

Prone to love You, Lord, I feel it,
Prone to serve the God I love;
Here's my heart, Lord, take and seal it,
Seal it for Thy courts above.

The power of the song "Come Thou Fount" is the revelation that we can always know His love. The song is about a journey to the cross. It is the good news that just keeps getting better. But the song is the beginning of a story, not the end. You see, the cross is the launching pad, the foundation, the slingshot that propels us into the victorious, miraculous, greater-works existence Jesus modeled and told us we had access to. The cross is only beautiful because of the empty tomb. We celebrate His death because of His resurrection. The power of love is perfected when sinners become saints. That was the whole point of Jesus's death and resurrection—that we would encounter love and become love.

Jesus never once was "prone to wander" or "prone to leave the God He loved." He came to the earth to settle that exact issue once and for all. He came to set us free, that we too might be transformed from "prone to wander" to "prone to love!"

If a person sings the line, "prone to wander," to tell the story of a life without Jesus, it is a powerful picture of a life-changing revelation. But when a believer sings those lyrics as a proclamation of the future, they are debilitating and destructive. While that line in the song is sound theology for the sinner, it is devastating theology for the saint.

Like my saint grandmother, I no longer sing "prone to wander." I can't, it's not true; my heavenly Father said so. Instead, when I sing this beautiful hymn, by faith I agree with how my Father sees me. I sing, "Prone to love You, Lord, I feel it, prone to serve the God I love." And I can't help but cry tears of joy while I sing this. Why? Because not only is it the cry of my heart, but because of my beautiful best friend Jesus, it's true! And how good is He for making it so. Thank You, Jesus!

Eva

I'm becoming like You, I'm becoming like You,
It's the cry of my heart, my King, that I'd display Your majesty.

My youngest child, Eva, recently turned five. As you can guess, Eva was named after my grandmother. My Eva is a firebrand of God's love. A couple days after her birthday party, Karen and I were in bed telling Madeleine, Ethan, and Eva stories. While Karen was reliving an Eva moment, I realized just how much our parenting had matured over the years, especially in how we discipline.

We have grown in our understanding that discipline is about revealing and releasing identity. For instance, if Eva lies about something, my greatest desire is not for her to learn and understand the consequences of lying. My greatest desire is for her to know that she is not a liar.

You see, my heavenly Father doesn't see her as a liar. So if she lies, she is not acting like how my Father sees her. He sees her as stunningly honest. As a parent, it is my privilege and charge to release her into that truth.

It doesn't mean we don't teach repentance; it's just that repentance isn't some ugly, self-loathing burden; it's not a form of punishment but a beautiful privilege. *Repent* simply means to change the way we think; it's an about-face. Repentance is about changing your mind until you are in agreement with God's. It's the good news!

In fact, that's what we tell our kids. When there is an issue where their hearts are self-focused, you will often hear Karen or me say, "Change the way you think." And because we have had the talk many times, our kids understand that what we are saying is, "Start thinking about yourself like your heavenly Father thinks about you." Here's the thing: if we learn to agree with how our heavenly Father sees us, we will start acting like it.

So while Karen and I lay in bed, she told me how the other day Eva had an intentionally forgetful moment and threw a tantrum. Karen sat down on the floor with her and kindly said, "Eva, change… what?" Eva, who had just been given a necklace from her Aunt Aimee that read, "I'm a world changer," looked at her mom and with a sudden sunny attitude and a mischievous grin, said, "The world?"

Change the world. Yep, that will work too! In fact, if you become brilliant at changing the way you think, you can't help but change the world.

I laughed with Karen as she told the story, and then we both agreed: Eva is correct—she is a world changer, that's how her heavenly Father sees her. That's how He sees you too. If you're unsure, change the way you think.

Our capacity to live a victorious, greater-works, world-changing life, is discovered in His love and our new nature. We are not Christian sinners; we are believing saints. We *must* learn to see ourselves from His perspective. This is what one of those philosopher types calls an ethic of necessity—it's not that we should or can, but that we must.

My grandmother Eva discovered at the age of ninety that she is not prone to wander but to love. My dad and mom in their late fifties are discovering that they too are prone to love. Karen and I in our thirties are discovering that we are not prone to wander but to love as well. And now our kids in their formative years are discovering that they are prone to love. This revelation has transformed my family. We are seeing God move miraculously in His great love for us. Seeing ourselves from our Father's perspective has changed our world and is beginning to change the world around us.

Praise the mount! I'm fixed upon it
Mount of Thy redeeming love.

Notes

1. These lines are taken from the hymn "There's a Wideness in God's Mercy," written by Frederick William Faber.
2. This is taken from the poem "Outwitted," by Edwin Markham.
3. For more information about this band, please visit http://www .bandofathousand.com.

Chapter Ten

LIVING ON THE LAM

Living on the Lam

It was a Sunday evening many years ago. I drove with a smile on my face and a happy feeling in my heart. I'd left Karen's family home an hour earlier after a beautiful weekend with my new love. I was almost back on campus—the Bible college that was snuggled in the wrinkles of the western New York landscape.

I sped around a corner, unaware of the police car until he raced past in the opposite direction. I reacted like anyone who is driving too fast; I hit the brakes. But it was too late. In my rearview mirror, I watched the cruiser disappear around the bend, but not before I saw brake lights and the nauseating flash of red and blue.

Mercy, that's what I need.

Have you ever been in a situation where you have to make a critical, split-second decision? You know, like, maybe there's a bomb and you are hovering over it with the wire snips. And let's say there's only five seconds left before all of Manhattan explodes into space, taking you and your dreams of making detective along with it.

This was kinda like that.

Mercy, that's what I need.

The instant I realized I was marked for judgment is the same moment that I saw the small gravel road a hundred feet ahead of me, to my right. It shot up a steep hill to God's country. I only had a second before the decision would pass me by.

It was like Bond took over my body. I watched as my hands whipped the steering wheel. Hardly slowing, I fishtailed my way onto the gravel road.

My powder-blue Toyota Tercel had never felt so alive. I put my foot to the floor, beads of sweat instantaneously appearing, as my compact savior climbed. "Come on, baby," I whispered, every muscle in my body tense. If I could clear the top of the hill before the cop passed the road he wouldn't know I'd turned and I could escape into the hills of western New York. I would change my name, live on the lam.

"Come on," I urged again, my eyes glued through my rearview mirror on the crossroads behind me. And then I was over. I was free and clear!

Mercy, that's what I needed.

I spent the next two hours driving the last thirty miles to campus on country roads with names like Moose Hill and Wiley while coming down off an adrenaline high that would not be equaled for years.

Mercy. I made my own.

Zacchaeus

I turn my face, to a blazing Son,
Your glory falls, Your Kingdom comes.

Zacchaeus was short. He was also a sinner—no relation. Zacchaeus was a man who was unfamiliar with love as evidenced by how he lived his life. He was a thief and he was also a tax collector—again, no relation. However, it seems he used his position of power to steal from the people in his hometown of Jericho.

One day, while perched in a tree in order to catch a glimpse of the arriving celebrity from Nazareth, Zacchaeus encountered the good news. He met Jesus, who loves both sinners and tax collectors—once again, no relation.

I imagine you know the story. It's found in Luke 19. It's also been wonderfully preserved in a children's song that employs the words *wee* and *little*. As Jesus is walking through the crowded street past Zacchaeus's tree, He looks up and greets the short man by name. "Zacchaeus, I must come to your house tonight!" And then Jesus, Love in human form, the Father perfectly revealed, goes to the wee little sinner's place for dinner.

You remember what happened next, right?

On the walk to Zacchaeus's house, Jesus made sure that the wee little sinner knew the full measure of his desperate wickedness. He pointed out Zacchaeus's sins and informed him that if he didn't change his ways, he was on the fast train to hell. Then, just in case Zacchaeus didn't understand, Jesus described hell. Finally, after Zacchaeus was convinced of his shame and unworthiness, Jesus told him God loved him.

But wait, there's more.

The best part of my fictional version of this walk to Zacchaeus's house is when the disciples handed out tracts to the passersby. The tracts were pretty clever. One side looked like money while the other had some inspirational writing on it, about the horrors of hell and how much God loves us.

Is my sarcasm too strong?

The fact is that not once did Jesus mention Zacchaeus's sinful ways. Not once did He chastise him, correct him, or challenge him. There was no shameful insinuation, no demeaning eye rolling, no suggestive mothering tone in Jesus's voice. Jesus's actions were loud and clear: "I love you and I am going to treat you the way My Father sees you."

If you spend time in God's presence, in worship, prayer, or in His Word, and you come away feeling shame or condemnation, you didn't get it from Him.

Living on the Lam...Again

Many years later I was driving again.

Karen was sleeping in the passenger seat next to me. We had visited her folks who now made their home in Virginia. We were heading home, back to western New York. I was irritated with my beautiful sleeping wife.

"Who does she think she is? I don't need her telling me to slow down every five seconds. I know how to drive a car; it's called the flow of traffic!" I thought as I sped along the Maryland freeway.

We'd just had a knock-down, drag-out, raised-voices, light-swearing fight over my speed—again! We had been married just over a year and I was getting pretty upset that she didn't know the unwritten universal rule that you can go nine miles over the speed limit and no cop is gonna pull you over! Everyone knows that!

I had just passed a large grouping of cars and trucks and was pulling into an open stretch of highway. I was going at least nine miles over the speed limit, when, across the grassy median, I saw the trooper heading south. I slammed on my brakes but it was too late. The moment I saw him was the same moment he saw me. His red and blues flashed and he pointed at me as he pulled into the grass and crossed the median. I flew past, our faded black Ford Tempo slowing as my foot momentarily lost the gas pedal.

Mercy, that's what I need.

Through my side mirror I watched the trooper as he idled on the northbound shoulder, waiting for my entourage of cars and trucks to pass him. I looked over at my sleeping wife, and suddenly it dawned on me that I was going to be married to her till death, which was possibly closer than I'd thought. And then I saw it, a mere quarter mile in front of me was an off-ramp. I looked in my rearview mirror, the trooper's car was now lost to sight behind all the vehicles. I couldn't see him but I knew he was there and he was coming for me.

James Bond, people.

I studied my rearview mirror all the way through the right-hand turn. "Come on, baby." I encouraged my Tempo as sweat beaded my brow. There were no red and blue lights to be seen as we cleared the highway and pulled into a gas station. My mind frenzied, my heart racing, I drove to a gas pump, putting the station between the interstate and the car.

Karen woke up.

Mercy, that's what I needed.

"Hey. Why are we stopping? Do we need gas already?" she asked.

I spoke calmly, like nothing was wrong. "I'm hungry." It was the truth. I get the munchies when I'm nervous.

"Then why have you pulled up to a pump?" she asked innocently.

"Dang, she was good," I thought, terrified. "Um, the gas prices are pretty good…I thought I'd fill it up." I lied. The gas prices were horrible in Maryland. But the lie was for the good. I didn't want her spooking. We would probably have to change our names and live on the lam.

Mercy, I made my own…again.

More Zacchaeus

I'm becoming like You, I'm becoming like You,
Let Your love be all I know, till Your glory becomes my own.

Mercy and grace are two sides of the same coin, both expressions of our Father's always-good love.

I have heard mercy and grace described like this: "Mercy is not getting what you deserve, and grace is getting what you don't deserve." I like that. I also think you could describe it this way: mercy reveals our Father and settles the issue of sin, while grace reveals our Father and settles the issue of identity.

Zacchaeus was a thief and a liar. He had a sinful nature and he was prone to wander. But one encounter with Love changed everything. When he saw and encountered Love, the sinner was transformed into a saint.

How did this happen? It's simple. Jesus was the Father's love revealed. Zacchaeus saw his Father's nature and embraced mercy. And then Zacchaeus saw himself through his Father's eyes and stepped into grace. Simple.

One evening with perfect Love and the sinner, now turned saint, declared that he would give more than half of what he owned to the poor and return four times what he stole. It was immediate transformation, salvation, the miraculous reformation that follows revelation. *"Today salvation has come to this house"* (Luke 19:9). That is the way Jesus described Zacchaeus's transformation.

Suddenly the sinner who had lived under the reproachful title of thief, the sinner who had lived under the shame of greed, and the sinner who had been unchanged by the condemnation of the entire town's disapproval was forever changed. One evening with perfect Love will do that.

Zacchaeus was living in one reality when he was introduced to a greater revelation. Zacchaeus was living in the very real measurements of earth when He was introduced to the measureless revelation of love. He encountered Love, saw himself from Love's perspective, repented, and decided to agree with how Love saw him. He got saved. Please get this: there was no shame, condemnation, or fear used to manipulate Zacchaeus into salvation. Jesus simply loved him—perfectly.

From man's perspective, Zacchaeus was a self-centered, small-minded, thieving liar. Through Love's eyes he was a generous, large-hearted believer who was capable of giving more than half of what he owned away. From his heavenly Father's perspective, Zacchaeus was supernaturally generous; he was prone to love. The moment he realized God saw him as generous, and the moment he repented and agreed with how God saw him, is the moment he became how God saw him—generous.

This was a miracle as big as blind eyes opening, as radical as cancer leaving. Jesus said this kind of miracle would be akin to a camel crawling through the eye of a needle. A rich man, who moments earlier lived his entire life for money, suddenly transformed into a generous man, completely free from the shackles and insecurities of greed. Simply amazing.

I am learning that what I think about myself should always be determined by what my heavenly Father thinks about me. I must see myself from His perspective. When I see myself through my Father's eyes, I become a saint capable of all the things that a sinner isn't.

This is how we become world changers. We simply encounter God's nature and agree with it. Every encounter I have ever had with God has been this way. He doesn't bring up my past weaknesses or my failures—there is no condemnation or shame. Instead, when I find myself in His presence, I am simply humbled by His good love for me.

It's not that I am unaware of some area in my life where I have "fallen short," but I am infinitely more aware of who He is, that He loves me, that He dwells in me! When God meets with me, I'm loved and inspired and empowered to become the saint that He sees.

"Be transformed by the renewing of your mind" (Rom. 12:2).

Transformation is birthed from the renewed mind. But how do we renew our mind?

"...it is God's kindness (goodness) that is leading you to repent" (Rom. 2:4 ISV).

Repent—change the way you think. The only way a mind is renewed is through an encounter with God's *kindness*, His *goodness*.

This encounter, this revelation, will transform us. We will become more like Him—prone to love.

Unbalanced Grace

If you want to read an amazing book on grace, read *The Ragamuffin Gospel*, or anything by Brennan Manning for that matter. Brennan is a hero of mine who faithfully banged the drums about God's love. He wrote about its beauty, its freedom, its transforming power. But my favorite thing about Brennan's writings is that he never felt compelled to balance grace.

I was hanging out with a friend the other day. He is in his mid-sixties. He is coming into such a wonderful revelation regarding our Father's love. He has lived most of his life enslaved to the harsh master known as *need*, but he is beginning to discover an always-good and loving Father. This beautiful revelation has entered his life in the form of grace.

For twenty minutes he spoke excitedly about how miraculously astonishing grace is. As he shared, I wholeheartedly encouraged and agreed with him. When he told me about the incredible freedom he was discovering through amazing grace, I laughed with him, reveling in the wonder. When he described how grace was empowering him to live free of sins that had haunted him his whole life, I grinned, nodded my head enthusiastically, and said, "Grace is good like that!"

He was well into praising how grace was changing the way he saw the people in his life when it happened. It's understandable; I've done it myself. Suddenly, like a fist to the jaw, he balanced it.

While describing the most beautiful revelation, while speaking with more passion and freedom than I had encountered in my eighteen years of knowing the man, he paused mid-sentence, and at absolute odds with what he had been sharing, he blurted out, "I know you can abuse it—grace."

And there it was. He balanced grace.

I could almost hear his thoughts: "Maybe I have gone too far, this grace thing is starting to sound too good to be true." I understood what happened. You see, grace can be a scary thing, especially when no one balances it.

It's not his fault. That ugly faux grace has been taught by those who have a greater fear of the world we live in than revelation of the Kingdom of heaven; those who focus more on need than love, on not sinning instead of becoming His righteousness (see 2 Cor. 5:21). When need trumps love, grace is a cheap parlor trick, empty powerless rhetoric.

My dad recently made a statement that amazed me. "Jason," he said, "if you teach grace to someone who knows the law and the question from Romans 6:1, 'Shall we go on sinning that grace may increase?' isn't raised, you didn't teach grace right."

"Should we keep on sinning so that God can show us more and more of His wonderful grace? Of course not!" (Rom. 6:1-2 NLT).

I understand that we can abuse the message of grace. I am aware that people can abuse people with a distortion of grace. The fourth verse in Jude describes how men can pervert and change the message of grace into a license to sin. But that's not what I am writing about. I am addressing the nature, the Person of grace. The fact is that if we truly encounter grace, we are transformed. If we truly know grace we will change the way we think, we will repent, ours minds will be renewed, we will be transformed and we won't want to sin.

Those that teach us that we can abuse grace don't fully know grace. That teaching looks at grace through the lens of need, the measurements of earth. It dumbs grace down to a commodity that can be traded for freedom or forgiveness or favor.

The message of balanced grace is a lie that enslaves us to live in the reality of need. A balanced grace is simply another way to control. If grace can be balanced, its power is neutered. And a powerless grace is a cruelty greater than no grace at all.

Grace won't be balanced! He is too perfect, too whole, too free, too just, too pure, too kind, too strong, too wild, too holy. Grace won't be belittled. Grace can't ever go bad or run out; He is the good news—always.

After my friend attempted to balance it, there was a dark and brooding silence that threatened to ruin everything. For just a moment we teetered on the brink of a faith crisis, but grace would have none of it. Right there on the verge of hopelessness, I told my friend the beautiful truth I am always growing in: "You can't abuse grace." Grace is not a tool to help monitor behavior; it is a revelation that empowers us to live in purity and freedom.

I went on to tell him that grace isn't too good to be true, but just the opposite—it's too good not to be true. Grace is unmerited favor. We can't do anything to earn it and we can't do anything to abuse it. Grace releases us to see ourselves from His perspective and empowers us to live in agreement with how He sees us, as saints of the Highest One.

Go and Sin No More

Oh grace, fire in my lungs,
All these songs the burning ones.

There was a woman caught in adultery. She was literally ripped naked from the bed. She was half chased, half dragged through the streets by angry tyrants with rocks. They meant to hurl them at the woman until her bones were broken and her flesh a bloody pulp. They meant to kill her for her sins. It's what she deserved!

Then Jesus, in all the Father's splendor, is thrust into the middle of the story. Can you picture it? The woman, weeping and afraid, is flung before Him. Then yanked to her feet, she's forced to stand. She tries to cover her nakedness. She won't meet His eyes; the condemnation is so great, her shame so real, her guilt so sure. She knows it, the angry mob knows it, even the disciples know it.

"The law says she should be stoned," the men scream, frothing at the mouth. "Need demands!"

And Jesus, our hero, does something so stunning it brings tears to our eyes. He reveals the Father's love—and it looks a lot like mercy.

"If any one of you is without sin, let him be the first to throw a stone at her" (John 8:7).

His statement resounds through the city streets, the nation, the world, and all the way up to heaven. "She will not get what she deserves because I am mercy."

> *At this, those who heard began to go away one at a time, the older ones first, until only Jesus was left, with the woman still standing there. Jesus straightened up and asked her, "Woman, where are they? Has no one condemned you?"*
>
> *"No one, sir," she said. "Then neither do I condemn you," Jesus declared* (John 8:9-11).

Mercy! It's beautiful—vast and immeasurable!

And if the story ended there, it would be worthy of the Good Book, worthy to be retold century upon century. But it didn't end there. Why? Because mercy by itself isn't enough.

Jesus didn't just come to set us free from sin. He came to release us into righteousness. He didn't just reveal the Father in all His mercy. He revealed the Father in all His grace. You see, Jesus never released mercy without following up with grace. In fact, mercy is incomplete without it.

The next thing Jesus says to the woman is just as beautiful, just as life changing as what's already been proclaimed. Jesus said, *"Go and sin no more"* (John 8:11).

And there's the grace, the power, and the wonder; the beauty and the immeasurable goodness of His glorious love.

It was mercy that set her free from what she deserved, but it was grace that transformed her into His likeness. It was mercy that forgave her, washed her clean, made her white as snow. But it was grace that empowered her to live as a pure daughter, a saint, and an overcomer.

I want to make this clear: not once, not ever, did Jesus release mercy without grace. He always empowers those He forgives. Mercy without grace is only half of the story. It's the Oreo cookie without the creamy center, it's Brad without Angelina, it's the beginning without an end. Mercy and grace are two sides of the same coin working perfectly together to reveal the fullness of His love—the whole story. Mercy covers sin, grace releases identity. Mercy sets us free, grace empowers us to become how He sees us. Mercy redeems, grace transforms.

The woman caught in adultery not only left set free, she left transformed. She received mercy *and* grace—the fullness of our Father's love! What had been her history did not have to be her future. Jesus changed the arc of her story; she was now a part of His story.

Regarding the woman caught in adultery, Jesus wasn't suggesting that she would never sin again, but He was saying, "You no longer have to be a sinner." I am convinced He was revealing why He had come, not just to forgive our sins but also to set us free from a sinful nature. Jesus was showing us that life no longer had to be about not sinning; instead, life could be about loving.

No longer must we live trying not to be bad; instead, in Him we can become good—heart, mind, and soul. No longer must we live enslaved to need; we are now invited into the revelation of love—both knowing and becoming! No longer must we live in the measurable limitations of earth, but we can live from the measureless revelation of heaven.

Living on the Lam...Again...Again

It was years later, and many years ago.

Let's cut to the chase, so to speak. I came over one rise just as the cop sped past me on the two-lane suburb road north of Jackson, Mississippi. He pointed at me, there was brief eye contact, and red and blue lights. As soon as his car disappeared behind me, I was turning left into a subdivision. I was shaken but not stirred. Bond, people, James Bond.

As I drove slowly through the subdivision, left turn, and then right, right, and then left, I wondered on possible names. Maybe we could be the Smiths or the Joneses. Karen would have to meet me in Switzerland with the kids and we'd have to live on the lam…again.

Mercy, that's what I need.

Half an hour later, as I pulled out of the subdivision and realized I was in the clear, breathing a sigh of relief I said the funniest thing: "Thank You, Jesus."

Yep, I actually thanked God. Then, hearing what I had just said, I started laughing.

I laughed for two reasons. The obvious was that God probably didn't help me in my escape. But second and more profoundly, I was just beginning to glimpse beyond mercy and into grace.

Grace, that's what I needed.

You see, most of my life has been spent recycling mercy. And because of this, there was little change, minimal transformation, just a hamster wheel of mercy.

When we live with a flawed understanding of love and believe we are prone to wander, then judgment is waiting around every corner and the best we can hope for is mercy. When we believe that grace can be balanced, then we find ourselves resenting the policeman that is driving around looking for speeders. We find ourselves slamming on our brakes every time God is near—a knee-jerk reaction to law. And when we think God's not looking, we find ourselves doing our best Bond impersonation.

But God isn't a cosmic policeman handing out tickets. He is a good Father. His love for us isn't motivated by what we do or don't do. He is not after our behavior. His mercy and grace aren't that cheap. They cost Him everything. He wants us to know who He is and how He sees us. He wants us to live in our identity as sons and daughters. He is after transformation.

If all we have is mercy, we will live with one eye always on the rearview mirror and one eye always looking for a place to hide out. Life without grace is a series of narrow escapes and recycled attempts at a clean conscience. Living on the lam is no way to live.

The Expectation of Grace

And as Your glory cloud descends,
Hey friends, it's time we got going.

"What shall we say, then? Shall we go on sinning so that grace may increase? By no means!" (Rom. 6:1-2).

There is a cheap grace being taught these days, a counterfeit grace with no true transformative power. This powerless grace is nothing more than a good feeling or hopeful sentiment.

A counterfeit grace is what we experience when we live from earth to heaven. It has no power and authority because it isn't birthed in the measureless revelation of the Father, but instead is a reaction to need.

I want to make it clear: while grace can't be balanced or abused, it does have powerful expectations. If we aren't becoming more like Jesus, if we aren't being transformed, we aren't living in grace.

Grace is not some license to sin.

Grace is the license to drive.

Chapter Eleven

SIN

I was wrapping up edits on the book when my good friend Josh said, "You have to write a chapter on sin."

I said, "No."

My Alarm Clock

It was the Christmas of 1984. I was ten years old. Aimee, Joel, and I all opened our identical, individually wrapped presents at the same time. I was old enough to know it meant we were all getting the same thing. "But what could it be?" I wondered excitedly.

I loved my alarm clock! It was progressive, white, high tech, small, science fiction, and digital—it was state of the art! Although my new BMX bike topped the gift list that year, the alarm clock was a close second. It was a good Christmas.

That alarm clock woke me for middle school, high school, and college. It cheered me on for 5:00 a.m. hockey practices and 6:00 a.m. coffee with friends. It woke me for road trips and international flights. It was a faithful companion long before I knew Karen. And after I got married, it came with me—its steady rhythms waking me countless mornings. Some of my best memories have been made with the help of my alarm clock.

Thirty years later the bike is long gone, but that white digital alarm clock is still with me. To this day it sits on my nightstand, its red numbers twinkling. It's hard to believe that strong, loyal, reliable machine has been waking me from slumber for over a quarter century. It has earned my respect.

And yet I hate my alarm clock. For thirty years that stupid thing has buzzed in my ear, forcing me to abandon the sweetness of sleep. The noxious arrogance of the vile sound assaults my spirit with its graceless existence. Its grating tone is like the sound of a million forks scraping across a million plates, its soulless wailing cementing exhaustion into my very bones.

When it begins its blathering, I can't turn it off quick enough. There are mornings where I wake one minute before it raves and thank all that is holy I escaped the sound. Over the years I have heard it on a TV show or movie and found my mood darken instantly. I feel sick to my stomach. I don't know if there is any sound more annoying than that of my alarm clock.

So I respect my alarm clock, but mostly I hate it.

What about Sin?

We were all sitting around drinking magic bean juice and talking about God. It was a rainy coffee shop day.

"What about sin?" she interrupted rather forcefully.

I was sharing with about ten college students on the perfection of our Father's love. Imagine this book condensed into about an hour. She had started to get jittery when I began discussing how we are prone to love. I thought it was the coffee, but it wasn't.

"What about sin?" I queried.

"Are you suggesting we can't sin?" she asked incredulously.

"No," I responded.

"Sin has consequences! You can't just ignore it! If you smoke, don't be shocked when you get cancer!" She was practically yelling at this point.

I don't know why she picked the sin of smoking as an example. I think she was just so upset about my seemingly unconcerned inattention to the issue of sin that she had to say something and smoking was the winner. But her point stood: *"For the wages of sin is death..."* (Rom. 6:23). It says so in my Bible and in hers. And death is a serious problem.

I said, "I am not ignoring sin. I am celebrating the absolute power of mercy and grace. I am not suggesting that there are no consequences or that lives aren't destroyed by sin, but I am suggesting love trumps *every* need. I am not proposing that behavior isn't important, but I am proposing that behavior follows identity. I am not focused on sin because sin is no longer the point; it hasn't been for two thousand years. The point is life."

It's very true: *"For the wages of sin is death but the gift of God is eternal life in Christ Jesus our Lord"* (Rom. 6:23).

That "but" is the game changer. It transitions our story, it changes the focus from law to love, judgment to mercy and grace, and death to life.

Who Sinned?

This is why I live and breath...

A Series of Coffee Shop Adventures. That would have been a good title for this book. By now some of you might think my life revolves around coffee and that's not far from the truth...

I was sitting at a Starbucks, happily drinking magic bean juice with a pastor friend. We were talking about mercy and grace and what Jesus's death and resurrection meant for our new nature when he pointedly asked me a question: "Are you saying you can go a day without sinning?" Hidden behind the healing sounds of pulled espresso shots and milk steaming, Mumford & Sons was setting the mood.

Love; it will not betray you,
Dismay or enslave you, it will set you free,
Be more like the man you were meant to be.[1]

Without hesitation I answered his question, "I haven't thought about it, but I sure hope so."

Oh, man! The look on his face...you would have thought I'd told him I was the love child of Hitler and Bin Laden.

Before his shock could turn to anger, I said, "I think your question is flawed—the premise is wrong. Your question suggests that the point of my life is to not sin. But I believe the point of my life is to know His love and become transformed. I am not saying I can't sin, I am not even saying I haven't sinned today, I'm just saying that it's the wrong focus."

Then I told him the same Jesus story I had shared months earlier at another coffee shop with some college students, one who was particularly concerned about smoking.

Jesus was walking down the street with His disciples when they came across a blind fella. His disciples asked,

"Rabbi, who sinned: this man or his parents, causing him to be born blind?"

Jesus said, "You're asking the wrong question. You're looking for someone to blame. There is no such cause-effect here. Look instead for what God can do..." (John 9:1-3 MSG).

It wasn't that Jesus didn't acknowledge sin; He just knew that the answer to the issue of sin didn't lie in the study of who sinned, but in a revelation of Dad.

The New International Version reads, *"Neither this man nor his parents sinned, but this happened so that the work of God might be displayed in his life."*

I'm convinced that Jesus sees every question raised by sin and death as an opportunity for love to be revealed. Every tragedy and every bondage is an opportunity for the Father's love to trump need.

Please understand me: Jesus was not saying that sin isn't a problem or that it doesn't lead to death. Nor was He suggesting that the blind fella had lived a perfect life or that his parents hadn't fallen short. He was simply saying that the focus is no longer on who had sinned, but instead on "Who loves you? That's right—God."

Everyone knows sin is a problem. The handful of people with Jesus and the millions who have read this story since know that the blind fella and his parents weren't without sin. More than likely, they had even sinned that day. But Jesus wasn't focused on the problem. He was the living, walking, talking measureless solution.

Think about it like this. Adam and Eve were both born perfect. As perfect, I imagine they had perfect twenty-twenty vision. The point is that we were created to see, it's in our original design. Blindness is the result of the fall. It didn't exist before sin and death entered the world.

For the blind fella, the result of sin in the world was devastating. In the day and culture he lived, blindness was directly connected to sin. In the day and culture he lived, blindness was a shame that stranded you as a hopeless beggar. Blindness was a life-and-death problem.

The question of sin dominated the reality and conversation of Jesus's day. It was the focus, it was the problem, and it was the separation from our Father's always-good transforming love.

Unfortunately, even after Jesus died and rose, even after Jesus declared, "It is finished," even after the veil was torn, even after we have been seated with Him in heavenly places to live from the measureless, even after we have been invited to change the focus, most believers still want to know who sinned so they can pin the tail on the appropriate donkey.

For some reason, we like that pinning stuff.

Identity > Behavior

Remember me, Jesus, here while I sing.

"Simon, Simon, behold, Satan demanded to have you, that he might sift you like wheat, but I have prayed for you, that your faith may not fail. And when you have turned again, strengthen your brothers."

These are some of the last instructions Jesus gives before going to the cross.

Peter's response? *"Lord, I am ready to go with You to prison and to death"* (Luke 22:33).

I love Peter's response—it's beautiful. Peter was ready to die for Jesus. You know, many years later Peter actually does die for Jesus. But he wasn't truly ready yet.

Jesus responds, *"I tell you, Peter, before the rooster crows today, you will deny three times that you know Me"* (Luke 22:34).

This conversation fascinated and confused me for years until I realized that Jesus said one thing and Peter heard something else. Jesus essentially said, "Pete, I'm praying your faith won't fail," and Peter heard, "Pete, I am praying that you don't fail."

Jesus wasn't praying Peter wouldn't sin or fail—that wasn't His focus. Jesus was praying that after Peter gave his life in his own strength, after Peter radically misunderstood the situation, after Peter tried to murder someone in Jesus's name, after Peter lived through the pain of three times denying the One he loved, after Peter lived through the death of his Teacher and Friend, after Peter lived under the soul-crushing guilt, the life-threatening shame, the horror of condemnation, the misery of anxiety, and the power of fear, after

Peter sinned and absolutely failed, that he would still believe Jesus loved him.

Faith believes His love is greater still.

This interaction between Jesus and Peter was not about Peter's capacity to sin; it was about Peter's capacity to believe that Jesus's love was greater than any sin. The focus was changing, the story was shifting, the reality of heaven was invading the reality of earth. Sinners were being given access to His righteousness, slaves were being transformed into sons and daughters.

Jesus was going to the cross so Peter could know the Father like He did and have access to the absolute power and authority of love. The cross would become the door through which Peter could know the redemption of mercy and the transformative power of grace.

Please get this: Jesus was praying and contending for Peter's identity, not his behavior. I'm convinced the Christian life is not a measurement of good behavior, but instead is full access to a measureless love that transforms. It's not about our failures, it's not even about our sin; it's about love, knowing and becoming.

Many days later, the resurrected Jesus walked a beach with His good friend Peter. Faith was restored through a revelation of love and Peter was transformed. On that beach, Jesus told Peter he would one day die for Him. Peter was ready now, his salvation secured and his revelation true.

Where Is Your Faith?

Everything I have is yours, all that I can give,
If you feel you're drowning son, it's My love you're drowning in.

Years ago I met regularly with a fella for counseling regarding, as he put it, his "battle with sin." Once a week I would tell him that his greatest battle wasn't with sin but the lie that he was a sinner. He strongly disagreed with me. For several months I walked him through Scripture and prayed the Father's good love over him. For several months I revealed to him the wonders of mercy and grace. And every time we met, I would challenge that his greatest battle wasn't sin but the lie that he was a sinner. He would disagree more strongly than when we last met and then reveal all the evidence he'd gathered to support his position. He was a sinner, period.

Finally I told him there was no reason to meet any more. When he asked why, I said, "You have more faith in your ability to sin than God's ability to make you righteous."

The truth sets you free. We kept meeting.

But his story is much like many of ours, isn't it? Before the miracle of his salvation, he behaved as a sinner and he was good at it. But after he was saved, he discovered that he was still pretty good at sinning. And that raised a question, "Why can't I get free?" And if the answer is, "Because you are still a sinner," well, that's not an answer at all, is it?

If our understanding isn't correct regarding the finished work of the cross, then the walls that once made our prison before Christ will be the walls we superimpose over our Christ walk.

Many of us still associate with God through the lens of a sinful nature even after we have been saved—delivered, redeemed, healed, and restored. Even after we have been saved—spiritually, mentally, and physically.

> But because of His great love for us, God, who is rich in mercy, made us alive with Christ even when we were dead in transgressions—it is by grace you have been saved (Ephesians 2:4-5).

This verse says it all. We *were* sinners is past tense. But we *have been* saved by grace is present-future.

"For the Son of Man came to seek and save what was lost" (Luke 19:10).

When we invited Jesus into our hearts, He restored that which was lost. We once again became spotless. Once again we could have communion with our Father. Salvation is the most beautiful of life's miracles. We once were dead, now we're alive. Alive, I tell you.

Grasshoppers

No more fear at every turn,
No more questioning what You have done.

The headline was brilliant, journalism at it's finest: "We Are but Grasshoppers in Their Sight!" And ten out of the twelve investigative reporters agreed, this was the best angle for the story (see Numbers 13–14).

Moses had sent spies into the land promised by God—twelve investigative reporters. They all returned. Like every good reporter, these men lived for the moment they could give personal commentary.

"The land flowed with milk and honey," they all said. It was lush and beautiful and an all-around wonderful place to live. In this they were all in agreement. However, the report didn't end there. The spies let Moses know that there were rather large people who lived in the land, and these people would probably not want to share. They would likely try to kill anyone who attempted to take it.

Now ten of the twelve spies went on to focus their report on the size of the land's inhabitants. "They are giants," they said. "And we are but grasshoppers in their sight." And with this bias as the cornerstone of their report, the consensus was that the land was unconquerable.

However, there were two spies who understood that the land was their inheritance. They saw the land through God's eyes. They saw the land from heaven's perspective—a superior revelation, a Holy Spirit bias—and their commentary reflected it. While they acknowledged the giants dwelling there, their focus was on the size of their God. "We can take this land," they said.

There is no such thing as being unbiased. There is truth that sets you free and then there is everything else. We don't need unbiased media, organizations, or churches. We need a revelation of love. The two spies who reported from God's perspective were biased. So were the other ten reporters. The bias is very important, it either empowers or enslaves.

There were two ways to report on the Promised Land: from the limitation of man's perspective or from the measureless revelation of God's. These are always the two perspectives we must choose from when it comes to life and what we believe about the finished work of the cross.

And in life, we know we are influenced by an inferior reality if fear dictates how we act regarding the giants that are in the land. We know we are influenced by an inferior reality if fear seems like wisdom. The ten spies were operating from an inferior bias—in other words, from a lie.

There was destructive power in the untrue commentary, "We are but grasshoppers." It turned the beautiful miracle of manna into welfare and produced a generation of manna-eating survivors. Manna was God's idea. And like all God's ideas, it was a good one, but He never intended it to become a way of life.

Those ten spies and their lie kept an entire generation from their promise. They condemned their people, their fathers and mothers, brothers and sisters, sons and daughters, to a helpless wilderness existence. They reported from an inferior reality, they missed the truth, and in so doing neutered their people and limited an entire generation's impact on the world. The Kingdom was not expanded in their lifetime.

Why Can't I Get Free?

Why can't I get free? Well, I would like to suggest that it starts with what we believe. If sin is the giant and we are the grasshoppers, then we have the wrong focus. If we enslave ourselves to a lie regarding the finished work of the cross, we will live in the relative poverty of manna. And we'll always be grasshoppers.

Behave

If we aren't sure in the perfection of our Father's always-good love, we can't become sure in our new identity as saints. If we can't become sure in our new identity as saints, then we will need to have our behavior monitored. If we need to have our behavior monitored, we will need to serve a controlling God. This completely undermines the cross. I kid you not.

In a world where sin is greater than love, there has to be laws and rules and police and armies and prisons to enforce and control behavior. Need demands that our whole society be structured around agreed-upon behavior.

When our focus is on not sinning, our understanding of the enemy is greater than our revelation of God's love. Christians should never live more afraid of failing God than revealing love. If our ability to sin is greater than His ability to make us righteous, we have undermined the power of the cross.

When we live in a rule-based relationship with God, we will feel insecure by the truth that in Christ we aren't sinners. When our relationship with Love is behavior-based, we will become apprehensive by the idea that sin is not the focus.

"If you smoke, don't be shocked when you get cancer." The fact is that has to be said when sin is the focus. But you know, our Father's love trumps cancer, even when the cancer is the result of the sin of smoking.

Discovering His Good Pleasure

There is a love beyond understanding; there is a grace that consumes,
There is a freedom found in surrender, my sacrifice, my song to You.

I was meeting with another fella recently who was convinced he was a sinner. He had proof and all the sad fruit, a broken marriage and hurting kids. He had asked God to forgive him but hadn't repented. He still believed he was prone to sin and he was hoping God could control him.

I asked, "When's the last time you felt God's love, His pleasure?"

He started to give me the correct answer, "I know God loves me…"

I gently cut him off. "I didn't ask for the right answer. When is the last time you felt God's absolute joy and laughter over your life? When was the last time you knew to your very bones that He was absolutely in love with you?"

He looked at me a little confused and he started to give me the correct answer again, "God is love. I know He loves…"

I interrupted again, "I didn't ask for a Scripture and I'm not looking for what you know here," pointing to my head. "When is the last time you experienced to the core of your being His unquestionable pleasure, His joy, His overwhelming love for you here?" I pointed to my heart.

He began to look back through his life. He went years back before he looked up, teary eyes, and said, "I can't remember."

"Well, that's where the problem started," I said.

He nodded in shameful agreement. He still didn't get it.

Then I asked him a question, which to him, considering the context of our meeting, probably seemed ridiculous. "Is He pleased with you right now?" He began to cry. "No."

"Are you sure?" I asked.

"How can He be pleased with me right now?"

"Ask Him how He sees you," I said, smiling with tears in my eyes. "I promise you, it's good news."

We spent the next half an hour discovering the good news. He is forgiven and it is his Father's good pleasure to give him the Kingdom (see Luke 12:32), the finished work of the cross.

For believers, sin is the crisis of identity. It separates us from who He is and how He sees us. But when we live in a revelation of His good pleasure, sin has no chance to separate us from our Father.

Turn the Stupid Thing Off

I'd like to propose that the news we often get these days is being reported and commentated on by those ten spies. If you listen closely, you will hear the newscaster, your neighbor, your workmate, and sometimes even the preacher say, "We are but grasshoppers." Or something very close to that.

If you are getting your information from the ten fearful, "grasshopper" spies, find a new news source. If, when you are finished listening to a commentary, you feel inadequate, fearful, or overwhelmed, find a new source. If after you've spent time with a friend, you feel insecure and hopeless, then find a new friend. If after you hear preaching you feel shame or condemnation, find a new preacher.

What I am trying to say is, "Turn the stupid thing off." Not one of us has to believe the liar that tells us we are but grasshoppers.

"Thy Kingdom come..." We are created to live from heaven's perspective. We are designed to see the world through His eyes.

How do we know when we are living from His perspective? We hope, we dream, we envision, we give, we risk. You see, from heaven's perspective we aren't helpless, hopeless sinners, we are the righteous giants meant to take the land.

The fact is that we all provide commentary. Personally, I want to be with the spies who got it right, the one who said, "We can take it."

I want to be the kind of believer who reports from heaven's measureless perspective, a son who knows and is absolutely sure in his heavenly Father's always-good love. I want to run with the saints who focus on love and not on who sinned. I want to journey with those who believe all impossibilities are possible with Him. I want to be a hope bringer who invades in the power of the resurrection.

Jesus commissioned, *"As you go, preach this message: 'The kingdom of heaven is near.' Heal the sick, raise the dead, cleanse those who have leprosy, drive out demons. Freely you have received, freely give"* (Matt. 10:7-8).

What's that mean? It means we are not grasshoppers; we are giants with all the authority and power of an open heaven. Stop focusing on the alarm clock. His Kingdom has come and is coming!

Conclusion

When my friend Josh suggested I needed to address sin in this book, my first thought was, "The whole book addresses it. Every word written is an invitation into our Father's love and our new identity as His sons and daughters."

I hated the idea of focusing on something that is no longer the focus.

But life is a journey, a daily revealing of the perfection of love, a constant invitation to move from slavery to freedom in a moment and then walk it out. Our mind is in the process of being renewed and while transformation can be instant, it's also continually expanding.

There is no better journey than this one—the journey from slavery to sonship, from need to love, from the measurable to the measureless.

I am convinced that if we lean into the revelation that our Father's love is always good and He is our righteousness, we will become transformed into His righteousness, and the whole world will know it. And the whole world will be transformed.

So that's my chapter on sin. Thanks, Josh!

Note

1.   These lyrics are from the song "Sigh No More" from the album by the same name by Mumford & Sons.

Chapter Twelve

WELL DONE

The Tire

Let's go find this Kingdom come, well done.

"Father, are we doing the right thing?" I asked for at least the thousandth time. We had stepped away from business nearly three months earlier. Karen was faithfully teaching our kids and I was faithfully finishing up my last book, *Surrendered and Untamed*. It was what we felt led to do. While we didn't have any idea how provision would come, we were trusting. We had just received our last paycheck. It barely took care of the month and that didn't include our mortgage, which was already two weeks late.

We were learning how to live in need and not be desperate.

"Father, I trust we haven't missed You. I won't be desperate about our finances but… well, I trust You." I prayed as confidently as I could.

The song "Swim Until You Can't See Land" by Frightened Rabbit was playing through my minivan's audiocassette adapter—a black tape with a cord off the end that ran to the headphone jack of my phone—very high tech.

Swim until you can't see land. It's a great description of faith and was an accurate narrative for this trip.

I was driving to meet some pastor friends I felt God had connected me to. They were gathering for the day to pray and encourage each other. I was doing about sixty miles per hour on two front tires I had no business driving on. The extra money I was dropping on gas and food to spend the day with these pastors was foolish. Actually, it was stupid.

"God, am I being stupid? My kids will want to eat next week. Father, I am not desperate. I trust You, but what are we doing?"

I felt Him respond to my heart with, "Do you have enough money for today?"

"Well, yes," I conceded. "But I need tires!"

He seemed unconcerned with both my plight and my tone. He responded to my heart by adding to His last question, "Do you have money for tires today?"

"Barely," I said, as the feeling of desperation tried to make an appearance.

"Then go get tires," He said to my heart.

Swim until you can't see land…

After the meeting I drove in to a service center where I was told two tires would cost $240 installed. So I left in search of a Wal-Mart. I found one. I parked in the back lot, walked into the service area, and bought the cheapest tires available—$140 for two tires mounted. I walked back out to the van and parked it in the service lane directly in front of the garage doors. I got out of the van, handed the keys to the mechanic, and then stood next to him. My mouth was open as we watched the front driver-side tire deflate.

"Do you see that?" I asked the mechanic incredulously.

"Yeah," he said, shaking his head, eyes glued to the tire. Then he smiled and said, "You got somebody driving with you, man!"

"Yes, I do," I replied, smiling calmly—not a desperate bone in my body.

As I walked across the parking lot to wait at the Starbucks that offered free Wi-Fi, I asked God, "What does it mean?"

Without hesitation, He responded to my heart, "I got your back."

As I walked, there were tears. There is nothing so sweet as hearing your Dad say, "Son, I got you."

As I thanked my Father for His goodness, I also smiled while reliving one of the thoughts that shot through my mind while the tire was deflating. It's a funny thought, and one that every person who has been tight in the wallet has had.

"I got every last moment out of that tire."

There was an immense sense of satisfaction with that thought. I hadn't wasted even an ounce of rubber. I had taken all the ground that tire could handle—even to the last foot. I used it completely. It served me to its absolute last breath.

Reliving that feeling, I said out loud, "Well done, tire." And I laughed with my Father as I walked.

I once heard Bill Johnson give a message in which he said that his entire life is being lived for a three-second moment with God. He figures that's about how long it takes for God to say, "Well done, good and faithful servant." I love that. I am also living for those three seconds.

It is my sincerest prayer that when I see my Father in heaven, He will have the same satisfied thought I had about my tire. "I got everything out of Jason. I had him, heart, soul, mind, and strength, to the absolute last. He took every piece of ground, every mile, every inch he was destined to take. He gave all—well done."

I think we all want to hear that. We all want to be world changers for our Dad. We all desire to be great sons and daughters to our incredible Father. In our heart of hearts we want to hear Him say, "You are My son, My daughter, and I am well pleased with you—well done!"

It's in our DNA to live for the pleasure of our Father. We are created to change the world, to transform darkness to light. We are designed to see the lost found, the poor rich, the sick healed, the dead raised. We are created to do great things for our Dad.

We are designed to live a life of risk and trust, to do valiant acts of faith, to live out radical acts of surrender, to swim until we can't see land, all for the glory of our King so that when we get to heaven we will experience in those three beautiful seconds, those six stunning words: "Well done, good and faithful servant."

But what if the "well done" we get in heaven has nothing to do with…well, doing?

Try Harder

Have you tried to be a Christian without Jesus? I have. It sucks. Literally.

Nothing is doable in this Christian life. Not one thing. Not even sleeping. Seriously. There is no checklist, no set of principles, no structure, no format, no commandment by which we can successfully navigate our Christian faith. Of this I am quite convinced. So was the Father. That's why He sent His Son. Jesus came, lived, died, and rose again. He defeated death and the grave, and with it the try-harder gospel.

Before the cross, humanity lived enslaved to need, religion was the answer, and commandments the way of life—keep the rules, try harder.

But Jesus turned religion on its ear. And in the process He made it abundantly clear that we couldn't try hard enough.

He told us that if we were angry with another person, it was just like murder (see Matt. 5:21-22).

Don't get angry with people, okay…*I'll try.*

He said, *"I tell you that anyone who looks at a woman lustfully has already committed adultery with her in his heart"* (Matt. 5:28).

Okay, yeah…*I'll try.*

He said, *"Do not swear at all…"* (Matt. 5:34).

This is getting kinda nitpicky…but…*I'll try really hard!*

He said, *"Be perfect, therefore, as your heavenly Father is perfect"* (Matt. 5:48)… %#*@*!…I mean, darn it…

The New Testament is crazy full of these kinds of Scriptures. It's full of what appears to be impossibilities—"Be *joyful always; pray continually; give thanks in all circumstances…"* (1 Thess. 5:16-18), *"Be holy, because I am holy"* (1 Pet. 1:16), and *"Go now and leave your life of sin"* (John 8:11).

Then there's this one: *"As you go, preach this message: 'The kingdom of heaven is near.' Heal the sick, raise the dead, cleanse those who have leprosy, drive out demons. Freely you have received, freely give"* (Matt. 10:7-8).

Have you ever tried to heal the sick? What about raising the dead?

I would like to suggest that these weren't some convoluted metaphors for church attendance and Bible reading. These weren't principles for clean living. These weren't behavioral demands. But neither was Jesus suggesting.

I believe He was promising.

Jesus didn't live, die, and live again so we could try harder. He didn't rise just so we could join a church and live a well-behaved religious existence. He came and conquered so we could know and become sure in our Father's always-good love. He suffered and overcame so we could be transformed by His always-good love, so we might become the church that grabs hold of heaven and pulls it down, the measureless surpassing all measurements!

New Testament Christianity, the life lived on the other side of the cross, is not doable. We can't achieve a "well done" by trying harder.

And yet Jesus said, "Greater works shall you do" (see John 14:12). The fact is, we are called, created, designed, loved, and even commanded to do all of it.

Writing

I imagine that my book editors are nice people. I understand that they have a job to do. But it has seemed to me at times they don't truly appreciate the hours, days, months, or years I've spent writing, and then editing, then editing again, until every word is art, every thought an impartation...at least, that's the aim.

Nope, when they send back their edits, there is rarely any coddling or sensitivity to my emotional equity. There are simply notes in the margins—glaring ugly blemishes on my lovely manuscript. They read something like, "This paragraph is distracting, you don't need it." Or, "That doesn't work, try again." Or, "The publisher won't allow you to use that word." Or, and this is the worst, "This story doesn't lend strength to the message, find another."

Find another? Like I can just forget this one, like I can just come up with something else!

At first I might grumble a little at the editor's notes, something like, "You're the hard candy shell!" Then I may watch an episode of *Arrested Development*. After that it's possible that I go to the Buffalo Bills message boards and read the latest banter and commentary on my beloved Bills. From there I typically eat something, Oreos with milk is usually good. And of course, there is always magic bean juice. Then I will go for a run. Finally, I put my noise-cancelling headphones on, turn up M83, and begin to read the chapter again, this time keeping my editor's hurtful and helpful notes in mind.

By the time I'm finished, I often find myself begrudgingly in agreement. Then I do the hardest thing a writer ever has to do. I highlight the section, copy and paste it into another Word doc that will sit in a dusty corner of my MacBook until forgotten, and finally...push...delete.

But before any of this happens, before an editor ever gets my manuscript, I have already done my very best to hear from my first editor and best friend—the Holy Spirit. I really love Him and I trust Him. It's my sincerest desire that His heart is revealed in everything I write.

The point is that there is nothing in this book that isn't deliberate. Every word has been vetted, looked over, deleted, rewritten, discussed, and of course prayed over continually. The final edit, the one you hold in your hands, it's as close to mirroring my heart as we could make it. The stories that made the final cut are hopefully the ones that best capture the message.

I am not saying that everything I've written reveals our Father's love, but that's my intent. I'm not saying the book is brilliant, but that is my intent. It is my desire that my reader can fully engage and encounter Love. Even rabbit trails like this one are written to serve that end, and so...

I can't tell you how it was with the early Gospel writers—the four fellas that wrote about the life of Jesus. I don't know their editing process. Maybe instead of sitcoms and NFL message boards, it was weddings and a swim in the Dead Sea. Instead of Oreo's and coffee, it was figs and wine. Instead of an album by M83, it was the cinematic gem *Fiddler on the Roof.* But one thing I'm confident of, we shared an editor and the same end goal—to be inspired by the Holy Spirit and reveal our Father's love.

By the way, I'm not suggesting that you are holding a fifth gospel, I am simply pointing out that the four fellas who wrote about the life of Jesus were every bit as intentional as I've been—even more so. When they sat down at their MacBook, like myself, they tried to write the best stories, the ones that most captured Jesus and revealed the Father.

Now here is what astounds me. While Jesus lived on earth for thirty-three years, perfectly revealing the Father's love, almost every story we have about Him takes place in the last three years of His life. In the first thirty, outside of His birth, we have only the one story from when He was twelve. Only one story made the final edit.

Think about it like this: for thirty years Jesus was the Father perfectly revealed and only a handful of people knew it. It's a crazy thought that the Creator of the universe, Love in human form, the answer to the question that is burning in the heart of every man, woman, and child, walked and talked on planet earth for the first thirty years of His life as the Father perfectly revealed and hardly anyone knew it.

I imagine Jesus probably did some cool stuff in His first thirty years, but we don't know about any of it. And there is a reason we don't know about it. It didn't get written down. Apparently the editor said that those stories weren't worthy of the final manuscript. They didn't make the cut.

While I am not suggesting that the stories of Jesus's youth weren't noteworthy to the Father, I am suggesting that those who wrote the books looked back over Jesus's life and, with the guidance of the Holy Spirit, determined that the best stories took place after Jesus came up out of the water, after He was baptized.

Most biographers endeavor to give the reader a peek into the formative years. They're called the "formative years" for a reason. And yet Jesus's early childhood stories are strangely absent. All four writers who chronicled the life of Jesus seemed to feel that the noteworthy stuff was what He did and said after His baptism.

My point? Because of this apparent lack of info, the tendency for us is to assume that those first thirty years were less significant then the last three. But I'd like to suggest that the Father had a completely different perspective.

Thirty Years Becoming Sure

When Your love is all I know, well done.

Jesus walked the planet the last three years of His life telling people who He was and backing it up with signs and wonders. He actually told us we didn't have to believe that He was the Son of God if He didn't do miracles.

"Do not believe Me unless I do what My Father does" (John 10:37).

But for His first thirty years, Jesus, the Father revealed, perfect theology, perfect ministry, Love in human form, lived among humanity and only a handful of people knew it.

We might be tempted to think that Jesus's first thirty years were not as significant as the last three simply because we have no miracles to measure Him by. However, I think those first thirty years are the reason He lived like He did the last three.

And so we find Jesus at the age of thirty on the shores of the Jordan River where He meets John the Baptist and is submerged beneath the water. The heavens open, a dove descends, and a voice like thunder rumbles, *"This is My Son, whom I love; with Him I am well pleased"* (Matt. 3:17).

And the question has to be asked. Why was the Father pleased? What had Jesus done?

And that's just it—we don't know. But whatever it was, it sure blessed the Father.

I would like to suggest that Jesus spent those formative thirty years becoming sure in His Father's love.

For thirty years Jesus discovered His Father's nature, and then discovered more of His Father's nature, and then discovered more of His Father's nature. For 360 months Jesus knew His Father's love, and then knew more of His love and more of His love. For 1,560 weeks Jesus grew in wisdom and favor until the absolute goodness of His Father was so deeply interwoven into His heart that it was the only reality He knew, until He only saw, knew, and did the work of His Father. For 10,950 days Jesus became surer and surer and surer in His Father's always-good love.

And then, after all that, in the fullness of time, Jesus gets an "attaboy." Well pleased.

Jesus got a "well pleased" before He did anything! He got the "well pleased" before He turned water into wine, before He walked on water, before He made more food out of less. He got the "well pleased" before He healed the blind eye, the deaf ear, the lame, or before He cleansed the leper. He got the "well pleased" before He cast out demons and set people free. He got the "well pleased" before He raised the dead.

He got the "well pleased" before He went into the wilderness, before He raised up world-changing disciples, before He went to the cross, before He rose, before He saved all of humanity and set us free from slavery to need. He got a "well pleased" before He ascended and then descended in the form of the Holy Spirit to release us into a brand new, one-of-a-kind, intimate revelation of His perfect love.

I believe all the beautiful works He did over the last three years of His life were the evidence of the first thirty years of becoming sure in His Father's always-good love.

When we get to heaven and we get a "well pleased" or "well done," it *won't* be for how hard we tried, or even for what we did; it *will* be for how sure we became in our Father's love. The doing will simply be the evidence that we believed He loved us. I believe this with every bone in my body.

When I get to heaven, I'm expecting to hear a "well pleased" or "well done" or "attaboy, Jason," because I believe. I believe God loves me, and I am learning to live like it, more sure each day, prone to love.

Parable of the Talents

There was a master with three servants. He was going on a journey and he called them to himself and gave each of them a sum of money: *"To one he gave five talents of money, to another two talents, and to another one talent, each according to his own ability. Then he went on his journey"* (Matt. 25:15).

You have probably heard this story. It's found in Matthew 25 and told by Jesus. Eventually the master returns home to, as Jesus put it, "Settle accounts with them."

The first fella embraced mercy and made good on grace; he had turned his five talents into ten. *"His master replied, 'Well done, good and faithful servant! You have been faithful with a few things; I will put you in charge of many things. Come and share your master's happiness!'"* (Matt. 25:21).

The second fella had a similar experience, also doubling his gift of two talents into four. He got the same beautiful increase in favor from his master. He also heard those stunning words we are all living to hear, *"Well done, good and faithful servant"* (Matt. 25:23).

But the last fella, it didn't go so well for him. When he came before the master, he said something terribly sad: "Master, I knew you to be a harsh and hard man, reaping where you did not sow, and gathering where you had not scattered seed. So I was afraid, and I went and hid your talent in the ground. Here you have what is your own" (Matt. 25:24-25 paraphrase).

With that, the fella returned to the master the one talent he'd received. Sadly, this guy, he didn't get a well done. *"His master replied, 'You wicked, lazy servant! So you knew that I harvest where I have not sown and gather where I have not scattered seed'"* (Matt. 25:26). It was a question, one that reveals something pretty serious: the master will judge us by the revelation we choose to live from, by the master we choose to serve.

And that's just what happened. After telling the servant that at the very least he could have banked the money for interest, he takes the one talent and gives it to the one who now had ten. But it gets way worse for the faithless servant: *"Throw that worthless servant outside, into the darkness, where there will be weeping and gnashing of teeth"* (Matt. 25:30).

Wow, that's pretty harsh. I mean, the fella didn't make you money and he's sent to hell? Normally, if someone doesn't return on their investment, they get fired or demoted. In some cases, when a fella can't turn a profit, he will lose his house and maybe his possessions. In extreme cases, where criminal behavior is discovered, and depending on the culture, the fella may even go to jail. But I have never heard of someone being thrown into outer darkness with the gnashing and the weeping because he was worthless at turning a buck, because he was a bad steward. But that's how this story seems to go.

Faith—Trust and Risk

While faith often looks like risk, at its core it's about trust. You only risk to the extent that you trust. As my friend John Blase recently wrote: "When Jesus said 'follow Me,' what He meant was 'trust Me.'"

The faithful servants were the fellas who understood the true nature of the master—that he was good and he loved them. It was this revelation that set them free to trust and empowered them to risk. Faith, after all, is about believing that he only has goodness and love for us.

What do we know about the one fella that got it wrong? His faith was in a lie. He believed that the master was evil. This enslaved him to live in the harsh reality of need. He could not trust and therefore he could not risk.

If you believe the master is harsh, your trust is compromised and you are not empowered to risk. The unfaithful servant couldn't even risk in trusting a bank. The unfaithful servant served an unjust, harsh, and controlling fella who was impossible to satisfy.

"I knew you to be a harsh master," he said. Need is a harsh master.

The guy that got it wrong basically positioned himself to serve a harsh master instead of a loving Father. He positioned himself as a slave to need instead of a son of love, a dwarf instead of a giant.

Stewardship

The power of stewardship—that's the truth Jesus was revealing in this parable. But it wasn't the stewardship of what to do, but of what to believe.

Jesus didn't tell us what the faithful servants did to double their talents. He just described their reward—the "well done" we are all living for.

If stewardship is about what we do, Jesus was rather cruel not to explain the faithful servants' secrets to success. Seriously, did they invest in gold or silver? Oil? Did their profits have something to do with real estate? What was going on in the stock market during that time? Was it a bear market or bull? Or was it some other animal?

If the focus of stewardship is on the "doing," and success is defined by multiplication, then for those of us who aren't business savvy or don't fully understand the stock market, this story is practically a death sentence.

And yet somehow the stewardship message that is alive and well within the church today has been dumbed down to behaving better, doing more, and trying harder. Somehow, the "well done" the faithful servants received has become about measurements when it was always meant to reveal the measureless.

Heaven's Stewardship

He told us to heal those who need healing, to bind up
the broken hearted, and bring justice to the oppressed.
But we cannot do these things unless every aspect
of our lives is about drawing closer to Him.
—Joel Clark, Awake[1]

If stewardship is taught as a principle without a revelation of His measureless love, then stewardship is ultimately irrelevant. If love is not our foundation, if love is not the beginning, then love won't be the end. There will be no transformation, no heaven on earth. And if love isn't the end, what's the point?

Without a revelation of our Father's always-good love, we have nothing to steward. "Greater works shall you do" (see John 14:12)—that's the promise, that's the Christian life. Healing the sick, raising the dead, living as the answer to every controlling need this world demands...

It is impossible to steward the way Jesus has invited us to unless we know Love.

The parable of the talents is about stewardship. All three servants stewarded one thing—their revelation of the master.

The faithful servants got a "well done." The faithless servant got cast into outer darkness. That tells us that stewardship is about one thing: faith in the perfection of His always-good love.

Kingdom stewarding is about truly seeing the Father and living in response to our revelation. It has nothing to do with trying harder; in fact, it's easy. If you know Love, you become love. If you become love, you don't have to try to love, you just love. And when you love this way, you steward well.

The "well done" we will get in heaven is about faithfully stewarding our revelation of His love. If we do this, we will trust and risk and discover that five becomes ten, and ten becomes cities, and cities become nations.

The fact is, we are created and called to do all of the greater works Jesus promised. But it can never be accomplished by trying harder. The transformative, need-trumping, doing what Jesus promised is only available to those who have become sure in His love.

If we are sure in His love, then we are powerful in our stewardship.

Now I Just Let Him Love Me

It's easy to love You...

Several years ago Anthony and Mary Keith Skinner visited the Clark family. Anthony and Mary Keith are worshipers who know the love of God. Anthony is a dad, a singer/songwriter, and an author; and Mary Keith is a mom, a teacher, and an encourager. They are a lot of things, but mostly they are loved.

You know what was really refreshing about the Skinners' visit? They didn't visit us for them. That's not to say we aren't good company, because we're amazing. But they didn't come to receive; they came to give. They walked through the door and started loving us before the coffee was fully brewed. And you know what was amazing? It was easy; they didn't even have to try. People who have lived immersed in the Father's love, well, they love, they can't help it; they've become transformed, they have become love.

Karen and I have begun to live this way as well. We are daily becoming convinced in our Father's always-good love. And so we too are being transformed. You know what the best thing is about becoming love? You don't have to try to love; it's just the natural expression of one who is loved. All you have to do is walk through the door and before the coffee is fully brewed... well...done...

Love is an awesome thing. The more you know and experience, the more transformed into love you become. There is an ease that enters your life. Even in the midst of hardship there is a grace to live at rest—like Jesus when He slept through the storm.

When you are loved and you know it, you don't have to try not to sin, you don't have to beg God for breakthrough, you don't have to strive to obey, you don't have to work up your love for God, your wife, your kids, you neighbor, your coworker, or even your enemy.

Jesus was love. It wasn't hard for Him either. There was no striving. He didn't have to try. All He had to do was keep His eyes on His Dad.

We went to Queen City Church, a wonderful family of believers, to worship with the Skinners that Sunday night before they headed to their Nashville home. It was beautiful, sweet, and powerful. It was all those things for several reasons. First, as my friend Andy Squyres says, Anthony Skinner's voice is a million bucks. So there was that. But it was also beautiful, sweet, and powerful for a profoundly simpler reason: the Skinners weren't there for themselves; they were there for the Father... and for all of us.

Mid-strum, Anthony muted his strings and paused, "I used to try and love God, but now I just let Him love me."

Note

1.   For more information about Joel Clark and his book *Awake: Discover the Power of Your Story*, please visit http://joelnclark.com.

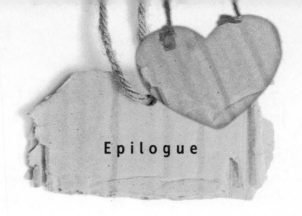

A FAMILY STORY

I come from a family that has faithfully said yes to God's love—a family of storytellers. Many of us dream in the language of music, film, art, and words. My family has its very own unique language. We have a history of love that defines our future. We dream, we hope, we pray, and we believe for a greater-works legacy of love, a world-changing revelation of His goodness.

Over the last years we have come to the belief that everyone should write, or in some form, capture the story. Not for a book deal, but to release a future and a hope—legacy. It's a reminder of where we have been and how good God was while we were there, even in the hard times—especially in the hard times. It's also about establishing a promise regarding where we are going. It's about God's goodness regarding what He has promised us as His kids, His people, His family. It's about legacy, about love, about remembering so we can know breakthrough, and breaking through so our kids can remember.

I write to capture the story for Madeleine, Ethan, and Eva, for Sage, Aliyah, and Juno, for Taylor, Hunter, and Gunner, and their kids and their kids' kids. I want to write them a legacy of the goodness of God. I want to record for them a story about the love of our Father. I want to build them a foundation upon which they can know love and in turn love. I want to write prophetically in the timeless voice of our heavenly Father speaking into their lives: "You have a great destiny, a holy purpose, and greater works shall you do!" I write so they will become sure and radically live and expand our Father's Kingdom.

This life is about leaving a legacy of love. It's about becoming and empowering; it's about chasing down, receiving, and passing on revelation for the generations today and the generations to come.

Like the apostle and writer John, my family, my friends, and I are discovering that the world can't contain the books of His always-good love. But we plan on spending our lives trying to write them…

We are writing, working, dreaming, praying, and living for a generation who has stopped living in the poverty of behavior-based Christianity, a generation baptized in powerful transformative grace.

We are writing, working, dreaming, praying, and living for a generation who believes they are giants, and when they experience disappointment, failure, or sin, none of it holds a candle to God's love.

We are writing, working, dreaming, praying, and living for a generation who won't wait for heaven when they die, but will live heaven to earth now, a generation who knows to their core they are loved and prone to love in the power and authority of all heaven.

We are writing, working, dreaming, praying, and living for a generation not defined by age but by a measureless revelation of love—beholding and becoming. We can see them, a generation so sure in the perfection of His love and so confident in how He sees them that the world is forever changed.

And we are a part of that generation.

Known, loved, and sure.

HEAVEN'S CRUSH

I love You, Lord, I lift my voice
To worship You, oh, my soul, rejoice
Take joy, my King, in what You hear
Let it be sweet, sweet, sweet to Your ears
I'm consumed 'neath heaven's crush
You are here, You're glorious
With joy, my King, I worship You
Let it be sweet, sweet, sweet to Your ears
It's easy to love You, it's easy to lift my voice
It's easy to raise a song and let my soul rejoice
It's easy to love You, it's easy to sing Your fame
I wanna give You all cause You're my everything

ABOUT THE AUTHOR

Jason Clark is a singer and songwriter, an author, a speaker, and a pastor.

Jason's passion is to know the love of God more each day. He lives to see a generation step into their identity as sons and daughters of the King and establish His Kingdom on earth as it is in heaven. He and his wife, Karen, live in North Carolina with their three children.

For more information on Jason's books or albums go to www.jasonclarkis.com.

ABOUT A FAMILY STORY

A Family Story is a relational community of my family and friends. We do life together, we dream and express God's love through our giftings and grace. We are a tribe of worshippers, dreamers, storytellers, and preachers. We are a community of moms and dads, brothers and sisters, daughters and sons, who simply want to live radically loved.

Our online home is www.afamilystory.org, where we can share what God is revealing through the lives of family and friends. There are some amazing books, albums, films, messages, and articles on this site, resources that will greatly encourage you as you journey into our Father's always-good love.

For more information on the community and ministry of my family and friends, you can go to www.afamilystory.org.

Many of the song lyrics featured in this book, *Prone to Love*, are from Jason Clark's New EP *Heaven's Crush*.

Heaven's Crush is available at
www.jasonclarkis.com and www.afamilystory.org

Praise for Jason's last album entitled,
Surrendered and Untamed:

"Both lyrically and instrumentally, Jason is wildly creative and builds an atmosphere of awe that lends itself to sincere worship.... (This album) will lead you as far into the presence as you are willing to go." —KEVAN BREITINGER